COMPUTERS
AND
EDUCATION

COMPUTERS
AND
EDUCATION

Other books in the At Issue series:

Alcohol Abuse
Animal Experimentation
Anorexia
The Attack on America: September 11, 2001
Biological and Chemical Weapons
Bulimia
The Central Intelligence Agency
Child Sexual Abuse in the Catholic Church
Cloning
Creationism vs. Evolution
Does Capital Punishment Deter Crime?
Drugs and Sports
Drunk Driving
The Ethics of Abortion
The Ethics of Genetic Engineering
The Ethics of Human Cloning
Heroin
Home Schooling
How Can Gun Violence Be Reduced?
How Should Prisons Treat Inmates?
Human Embryo Experimentation
Is Global Warming a Threat?
Islamic Fundamentalism
Is Media Violence a Problem?
Is the Death Penalty Fair?
Legalizing Drugs
Marijuana
Missile Defense
National Security
Nuclear and Toxic Waste
Nuclear Security
Organ Transplants
Performance-Enhancing Drugs
Physician-Assisted Suicide
Police Corruption
Professional Wrestling
Rain Forests
Satanism
School Shootings
Should Abortion Rights Be Restricted?
Should There Be Limits to Free Speech?
Teen Sex
Vaccinations
Video Games
What Encourages Gang Behavior?
What Is a Hate Crime?
White Supremacy Groups

COMPUTERS AND EDUCATION

James D. Torr, *Book Editor*

Daniel Leone, *President*
Bonnie Szumski, *Publisher*
Scott Barbour, *Managing Editor*
Helen Cothran, *Senior Editor*

GREENHAVEN
PRESS®

THOMSON
———*———
™
GALE

San Diego • Detroit • New York • San Francisco • Cleveland
New Haven, Conn. • Waterville, Maine • London • Munich

LIBRARY OF CONGRESS CATALOGING-IN-PUBLICATION DATA

Computers and education / James D. Torr, book editor.
    p. cm. — (At issue)
Includes bibliographical references and index.
ISBN 0-7377-1610-X (pbk. : alk. paper) — ISBN 0-7377-1609-6 (lib. bdg. : alk. paper)
    1. Computer-assisted instruction. I. Torr, James D., 1974– . II. At issue (San
Diego, Calif.)
LB1028.5 .C517 2003
371.33'4—dc21
                                      2002034657

Contents

		Page
Introduction		9
1.	Schools Should Adopt Computer-Assisted Education *Howard Gardner*	12
2.	Schools Should Not Adopt Computer-Assisted Education *Clifford Stoll*	16
3.	Computer-Assisted Education Can Enhance Learning *National Research Council*	22
4.	Computer-Assisted Education May Not Enhance Learning *Alison Armstrong and Charles Casement*	37
5.	Computers Can Make Students More Interested in Learning *Leslie Bennetts*	49
6.	Computer-Assisted Education Can Undermine Serious Study *Joanne K. Olson and Michael P. Clough*	56
7.	Computer-Assisted Education Benefits Young Children *The Children's Partnership*	66
8.	Computer-Assisted Education Does Not Benefit Young Children *Alliance for Childhood*	73
9.	Computer Literacy Is Vital to Students' Future Success *Diane Rezendes Khirallah*	78
10.	Traditional Literacy Is More Important than Computer Literacy to Students' Future Success *Susan B. Barnes*	85
11.	Computer-Assisted Education Could Radically Alter the Role of Teachers *Frederick Bennett*	93
12.	Computers Cannot Replace Teachers *Vivienne Collinson*	101
Organizations and Websites		113
Bibliography		117
Index		119

Introduction

The debate over the use of computers in public education dates back to at least 1983, when the federally appointed National Commission on Excellence in Education issued its report *A Nation at Risk*, which harshly criticized the failures of the U.S. educational system and tied them to the nation's economic problem: "Our once unchallenged preeminence in commerce, industry, science, and technological innovation is being overtaken by competitors throughout the world. . . . The educational foundations of our society are presently being eroded by a rising tide of mediocrity that threatens our very virtues as a Nation and a people." The report concluded, "We must dedicate ourselves to the reform of our educational system for the benefit of all."

The warnings of *A Nation at Risk* came at a time when Americans were beginning to embrace computer technology. IBM had just released the first personal computer in 1981; the company sold 6 million of them in 1983. In 1984, Apple Computer gained popularity after introducing the Macintosh, a personal computer that featured a novel, easy-to-use graphical user interface and a mouse in addition to a keyboard. The Internet and the World Wide Web would not gain popularity for another decade, but in the early 1980s Americans already felt that a social transformation was underway and that their children should be prepared for it. As the authors of *A Nation at Risk* put it, "Learning is the indispensable investment required for success in the 'information age' we are entering."

By 1988 more than half of all workers in the United States were using computers. The nation's school system followed this trend: According to *American Prospect* cofounder Paul Starr, "Between 1981 and 1991, the proportion of schools with computers rose from 18 percent to 98 percent, and the number of students per computer fell from 125 to 18." Elementary and middle schools purchased mostly Apple computers, while high schools favored DOS-, and later, Windows-based machines. And as computer technology became more advanced, so too did the educational software that was marketed to schools. Computer-assisted education (CAI) was, and still is, touted as a potentially revolutionary new means of learning. "PCs and general applications software made computing more flexible and easily adapted to different subjects and styles of teaching," writes Starr. He adds, "Unlike motion pictures, radio, and TV, computers were far more susceptible to both student-centered and teacher-defined activities."

In the early 1990s, the movement to use computers in the classroom was reinvigorated by the explosive growth of the Internet and the World Wide Web. Many parents and educators hoped that the Internet would enrich CAI and the overall educational experience by connecting classrooms to the outside world. Responding to this enthusiasm, in 1996 President Bill Clinton proposed federal funding to help bring computer and Internet technology into all classrooms by 2000. Congress allotted $2 billion to the Technology Literacy Fund in 1997, and this money helped bring the percentage of K–12 classrooms connected to the Internet from 3 percent in 1994 to 77 percent in 2000. Grants for integrating Internet technology into education were also a major part of the No Child Left Behind Act that President George W. Bush signed into law in January 2002.

The case for integrating computers into the classroom is summed up by a 2002 Department of Education report:

> The latest research and evaluation studies demonstrate that school improvement programs that employ technology for teaching and learning yield positive results for students and teachers. Given that many schools and classrooms have only recently gained access to technology for teaching and learning, the positive outcomes of these studies suggest a future for education that could be quite bright if the nation maintains its commitment to harnessing technology for education.
>
> The adoption of new and emerging technologies by schools and classrooms offers even more reason to be hopeful. With sufficient access and support, teachers will be better able to help their students comprehend difficult-to-understand concepts and engage in learning, provide their students with access to information and resources, and better meet their students' individual needs. If we take advantage of the opportunities presented to us, technology will enhance learning and improve student achievement for all students.

In addition, a 2002 National Policy Association report titled *Building a Digital Workforce: Confronting the Crisis* emphasizes the need to train students for a computer-dominated workplace. Echoing 1983's *A Nation at Risk*, the authors of *Building a Digital Workforce* write: "America has a workforce crisis. It has a sufficient supply of workers, but they lack adequate 21st Century IT [information technology] skills to fuel the information age economy. . . . Unless the country acts now to fill this gap, its competitiveness may be threatened."

Yet, from its very outset in the late 1970s and early 1980s, the movement to use computers in education has had its share of critics, many of whom simply don't believe the claims of technology enthusiasts. For technology skeptics, zealous claims about CAI echo Thomas Edison's 1922 prediction that "The motion picture is destined to revolutionize our educational system and . . . in a few years it will supplant largely, if not entirely, the use of textbooks." Motion pictures became primarily a media for entertainment rather than education, and critics charge that the same thing is happening to computers and the Internet.

The anti-technology viewpoint is presented in detail in books such as 1999's *High-Tech Heretic: Why Computers Don't Belong in the Classroom and Other Reflections by a Computer Contrarian*. Author Clifford Stoll argues against the conventional wisdom that students need to be computer literate to succeed in the workplace:

> What jobs will be around in 2100? Surprise! They're pretty much the same jobs available today: dentists, truck drivers, surgeons, ballet dancers, salespeople, entertainers, and school-

teachers. A century from now, there will still be movies stars, morticians, gardeners, forest rangers, and police officers. . . . Curious thing about all these jobs—none of them require computing.

But the main argument used by parents, teachers, and policy makers who oppose CAI is that the money that schools spend on computers could be better used for other things, primarily hiring more teachers. This view was expressed in 1998 by the National Science Board (NSB):

The fundamental dilemma of computer-based instruction and other IT-based educational technologies is that their cost-effectiveness compared to other forms of instruction— for example, smaller class sizes, self-paced learning, peer teaching, small group learning, innovative curricula, and in-class tutors—has never been proven.

The NSB is referring to the fact that widespread use of computers in education is less than two decades old, and research on its effectiveness is largely ambiguous.

Indeed, one thing that both sides of the computers-in-education debate agree on is that more research is needed to determine what educational techniques—computer-assisted or otherwise—are most beneficial for students. As Michael Dertouzos, author of *What Will Be: How the New World of Information Will Change Our Lives*, puts it, "We need to continually examine what succeeds and fails, and why. And we should do so before we deploy any technical approach on a grand scale." America's schools are the laboratories in which educators' many different experiments with CAI are being conducted.

The debate over computers in education is constantly evolving based on new research and technological advancements. Ultimately, decisions about whether and how to use computers in education will be made largely by individual communities and schools, based on their particular resources, needs, and goals. The viewpoints in *At Issue: Computers and Education* highlight the main arguments in the debate about whether CAI is good for the nation's school system as a whole.

1

Schools Should Adopt Computer-Assisted Education

Howard Gardner

Howard Gardner is a professor of cognition and education at the Harvard Graduate School of Education.

Schools are traditionally resistant to change, but they cannot ignore the ways in which computer technology is transforming society. Computer-assisted education will allow schools to design curricula that are individualized to each student. Outside the classroom, the easy availability of information on the Internet will increase individuals' ability to educate themselves and become lifelong learners. Finally, computer-enhanced education will be part of a larger transformation of education, which could include medical innovations that will enhance learning.

Technology has revolutionized the world in which schools operate. Now it's time for educators to catch up to change.

A human being miraculously transported from 1900 to our time would recognize much of what goes on in today's classrooms—the prevalent lecturing, the emphasis on drill, the decontextualized materials and activities ranging from basal readers to weekly spelling tests. With the possible exception of the church, few institutions have changed as little in fundamental ways as those charged with the formal education of the next generation.

Contrast this continuity with children's experiences outside the school walls. In modern society children have access to a range of media that would have seemed miraculous in an earlier era (and that still astonishes members of less industrialized societies): television, cellular phones, personal computers with CD-ROMs, fax machines, videodiscs, personal stereos, and still and video cameras.

The visitor from the past who would readily recognize today's classroom would have trouble relating to the out-of-school world of a 10-year-old today. I confess that I often experience such difficulties myself.

Schools—if not education generally—are inherently conservative in-stitutions. In large measure, I would defend this conservatism. But changes in our world are so rapid and so decisive that it will not be pos-sible for schools to remain as they were or simply to introduce a few su-perficial adjustments. Indeed, if schools do not change rapidly and radi-cally, they are likely to be replaced by other, more responsive (though perhaps less comfortable and less legitimate) institutions.

The transforming power of computers

The most important technological event of our time is the ascendancy of the computer. Computers already play a prominent role in many aspects of our lives, from transportation and communication to personal book-keeping and entertainment. Scarcely oblivious to these trends, many schools now have computers and networking capabilities. To some ex-tent, these technological appurtenances have been absorbed into the life of the school, though often they simply deliver the old lessons in a more convenient and efficient format.

In the future, however, education will be organized largely around the computer. Computers will permit a degree of individualization—per-sonalized coaching or tutoring—which in the past was available only to the rich. All students may receive a curriculum tailored to their needs, learning style, pace and profile of mastery, and record of success with ear-lier materials and lessons. Indeed, computer technology permits us to re-alize, for the first time, progressive educational ideas of "personalization" and "active, hands-on learning" for students all over the world.

In the future . . . education will be organized largely around the computer.

Computer technology puts all the information in the world at one's fingertips, quite literally. This is both a blessing and a curse. No longer do we have to spend long periods of time hunting down a source or a per-son—these can be found instantaneously. Soon we will not even have to type in an instruction in order to learn the capital of Montana, the pop-ulation of Korea, or Ohm's law; we will be able to simply ask a question out loud and the computer will print out or speak the answer. Thus people will achieve instant "cultural literacy."

Less happily, the Internet has no means of quality control; "anyone can play." Information and disinformation commingle comfortably and, as of yet, there are no reliable ways to distinguish sense from distortions and downright nonsense on the Net. Ethnographer Sherry Turkle tells about the young child who insists that "there are always riots when taxes go up" because that is the common wisdom embedded in the widely available game program, Sim City. Identifying the true, the beautiful, and the good—and which of these truths, beauties, or goods are worth know-ing—constitutes a formidable challenge.

It might be said, in response, that the world has always been filled with misinformation. True enough, but in the past educational authorities could at least choose their favorite texts (and proscribe others). Today's situation, with everyone having instant access to millions of sources, is unprecedented.

Artificial intelligence and virtual reality are two computer-related technologies that may cast a large shadow on education. Much of school planning may be done not by human agents but by programs created by human agents; and much of what was once accomplished by textbooks and occasional field trips will now be performed in virtual reality. One can ask: What is the truth value of materials prepared entirely by nonhuman entities?

Customizing education

In a turnabout from previous trends, the acquisition of credentials from accredited institutions may become less important. Individuals will be able to educate themselves (largely if not wholly) and to exhibit their mastery in a simulated setting. Why pay $120,000 to go to law school, if one can "read law" as in earlier times and then demonstrate one's legal skills via computer simulation? Or learn to fly a plane or conduct neurosurgery by similar means, for that matter?

Much of education in the past was calibrated to make sure that individuals could carry out a regular job, reliably, throughout their productive adult years. Nowadays, this assumption is doubly flawed. First, almost everything that can be handled algorithmically will be carried out by automata. Second, few people will remain in the same occupational niche for their whole lives; many will move frequently (either voluntarily or by necessity) from one niche, company, and sector of the economy to another.

The explosion of new and rapidly changing roles in the workplace complicates education in unprecedented ways. Most adult teachers and parents will not have experiences on which they can draw to prepare youngsters for a world in which they can expect to change jobs regularly. In the absence of precedent, youths will have to prepare themselves for rapidly changing "career paths" and life situations.

The further effects of technology

While computer-based teaching and curricula figure to be the dominant technological influence on education, other innovations will have impacts as well. Imaging technologies will permit study of students' brain activity and blood flow as they engage in various kinds of problem-solving or creative activities. No longer restricted to research, these findings about a student's "mental life" are likely to influence pedagogical approaches as well as his or her placement in special or mainstream educational settings.

Enhanced understanding of the genetic basis of learning and of various talents is also likely to intrude on the classroom. It may be possible to determine which youngsters are likely to advance quickly and which ones seem doomed to "uphill" school experiences; some authorities will insist that these findings be applied in specific cases, while others will strenuously object to any decisions made on the basis of genetic information. Drugs that purport to improve learning, memory, or motivation will become readily available. Teachers and parents may face ethical dilemmas that would in earlier times have been restricted to science fiction.

Finally, recent breakthroughs in biology and medicine may change education in the most radical ways. If individuals seek to "design" offspring through genetic engineering, or to alter the genetic endowment of an already existing person, or if human cloning becomes a reality as well as a possibility, then our definitions of what it means to be a human being, and to be a part of a human society, will be changed forever. Even the laws of evolution may have to be reconceived.

I have noted that education is conservative, and that this conservatism is not necessarily an evil. Indeed, with respect to the transmission of values and the mastery of certain notational systems and disciplines, a conservative approach may well be called for. Yet the explosion of knowledge and the ever-shifting cartography of disciplines call for close and fresh attention to curricular matters. And new and imaginative approaches will have to be developed if youths are to be prepared for the rapidly changing roles they can expect to assume.

2

Schools Should Not Adopt Computer-Assisted Education

Clifford Stoll

Clifford Stoll is the author of Silicon Snake Oil: Second Thoughts on the Information Highway *and* High-Tech Heretic: Why Computers Don't Belong in the Classroom and Other Reflections by a Computer Contrarian, *from which the following viewpoint is excerpted.*

In their rush to embrace computer-assisted education, too many schools have underestimated the enormous costs it involves. Schools across the country are opting to use their limited budgets to pay for Internet access and computers rather than better music programs, more English teachers, or improved scientific laboratory equipment. Moreover, the rapid pace of technology insures that schools will have to buy new computers every few years. Given the choice between buying more computers or hiring more or better teachers, schools should choose teachers.

What's the cost of computers in the classroom? Around the country, communities float thirty-year bond issues to buy computers which will be obsolete within five years. Wiring a school typically costs thousands of dollars per classroom; and it will have to be redone within a decade, as communications systems evolve. Classroom software has a surprisingly short life, as curriculum, computers, and educational climate change. Then there's the need for technical support—it's silly to expect English teachers to install and maintain the high school's file servers.

No question that computing is much cheaper than twenty years ago. Yet our schools don't magically get expanded budgets, although it seems as if technology grant money comes free for the asking.

No, there's a finite number of bucks available for education; pushing some into computing means less money for other programs. By insisting that we spend time and money on technological teaching tools, we implicitly reduce the amount of time and money spent on other programs.

The hidden cost of computers

Listen to Kathy Popp, technology coordinator for a small, rural community in south central Pennsylvania.

First, Ms. Popp recites the usual clichés: "Chestnut Ridge School District shares a vision with the surrounding community . . . that technology can be the catalyst and agent in changing the way teachers teach and the way students learn. Our vision sees technology as the great equalizer, in a playing field where unequal amounts of money are spent on educating children."

As the Amish leave that area, technology will become both cornucopia and equalizer. How'll they reach this utopia?

"Access and use of the Information Highway is part of this technology. But in order to purchase technology," Ms. Popp writes, "both teachers and district supplies have to be cut."

What? Given a choice between buying computers and hiring teachers, she picks the machines. Indeed, the Internet is so valuable to this rural district that "Workshops have even been held for the secretaries, aides, cooks, and janitors."

Cooks and janitors need Internet training? Do they expect cybercooking and electrocleaning? Ms. Popp continues: "The commitment of our school and community was evident when money was budgeted this school year for a 56 Kilobaud line. A high school teacher position was left unfilled, and supplies were cut. That's commitment to connectivity."

For the price of one less English teacher, her school district now boasts a medium-speed Internet link. In southern Pennsylvania, at least, browsing the Web takes precedence over learning how to write.

Which is more important: Internet or books? Computers or teachers? On-line access or a local clinic? Kathy Popp has no doubt: "We see access to unlimited use on the Information Highway as the books we don't have on our high school library shelves and the experts we don't have in a rural setting. We see it as a health resource in an area which is classified as medically underserved."

> *By insisting that we spend time and money on technological teaching tools, we implicitly reduce the amount of time and money spent on other programs.*

Faced with pressing educational and social problems, technology promoters first turn to the Internet. They're blind to other possible solutions, such as more teacher support, better teaching conditions, tighter discipline, more appropriate curricula, or recasting school goals. This obsession with computing tilts community activity as well. There's no reason to improve the library, start a health clinic, or open a community college. Just bring in the Internet.

Perhaps Ms. Popp feels that a half-baked electronic educational casserole is better than nothing. Without the Internet, her students might not be exposed to information which is simply unavailable in rural Pennsylvania.

Well sure, there's plenty on-line that can't be found in the Chestnut Ridge School District. But instead of exploiting what's available locally—the people, color, and history of the region—computer promoters press students to reach into the non-world of cyberspace. Seek answers from the net, not from a teacher or mentor. Build relationships via e-mail, not by meeting people. Explore the Web, not your own community.

Skewed priorities

What if your school can afford only one computer for a class of twenty-five students? No problem, says Peggy Ratsch, information technology specialist in Baltimore County Public Schools. According to *Education Technology News,* she says that if teachers can show they're using one machine well in the classroom, they are more likely to get funding for more. In other words, get the first computer so that you can get others. Presumably, the aim is every student behind a computer . . . but I doubt that will end Ms. Ratsch's money hunt. Technologists see technology as a solution, never as a problem.

For the cost of two dozen computers, you can equip a terrific high school physics lab.

Former president Bill Clinton announced that a computer in every classroom is a goal of education. Not a means, but a goal. What's wrong with this picture?

If technology is adopted as education's crown jewels, our classrooms naturally change their value structures. At Poly High School in Long Beach, California, the roof leaked big time, and rainwater dripped into the classrooms. What to do? Why, save the computers! The principal sent out a message that teachers could get plastic bags from the main office.

No thought that books, desks, or student projects might be worth saving. Certainly no suggestion that money might be better spent on a new roof which would last thirty years, rather than computers with maybe a five-year life span.

Massachusetts Institute of Technology (MIT) sociology professor Sherry Turkel also favors bringing computers into schools, though she recognizes the limitations. If you just drop a lot of computers into the classroom, "Nothing miraculous is going to happen." And for some areas, the computer isn't the best tool for teaching. "You need a teacher and a conversation to teach the beauty of poetry," she said.

What about science? Well, Professor Turkel's seven-year-old daughter was curious about magnets. The girl had a computer program about magnets but didn't really understand them. Then Professor Turkel bought a magnet for her daughter. "Once she was holding it in her hands, she got it," she said.

Wait a second. This child's in second grade, fluent in computing, yet hasn't played with magnets. What household provides a computer for a kid but not refrigerator magnets?

Same thing happens in schools. Classrooms get plenty of computers and software, but not such things as paper, crayons, blocks, and, yes, magnets. An ISDN line instead of an English teacher.

Here's an anonymous Canadian schoolteacher, quoted by K. Reil at the University of Victoria: "They can give us the ax, but they can spend thousands on computers. We have to fire our music coordinator, we have to fire our music teachers, and we have shitty libraries."

Next time a principal or school board member shows off a modern computer lab in eighth grade, ask this question: "What was in this room before these computers?" Here are the answers I got:

"We converted the library into the computer lab. With the multimedia encyclopedias, we no longer need as many books."

"Oh, we used to teach art in this room. But we don't anymore."

"This technology lab used to be our carpentry shop."

"A music studio . . ."

Computer labs are replacing scientific labs

And if you think computers only cut into school libraries and music programs, you should check out high school chemistry labs. The days of test tubes and Bunsen burners are fast disappearing, as school districts get scared of students handling chemicals. Too easy to spill acid, burn a finger, or build a bomb. With safety concerns driving up the cost of real chem labs, schools naturally turn to the high-tech solutions: computer simulations.

School chemistry software comes complete with pretty images of thermometers, pipets, and condensers. To simulate a titration, you type in commands, use a mouse to drag a simulated beaker across the screen, and then watch the effect on a simulated pH meter. Sure looks spiffy, but it ain't chemistry. It's simulated chemistry.

Visit the Science Magnet School in Buffalo, New York. Over near Humboldt Park, you'll find dozens of computers, complete with modems and high-resolution monitors. They sponsor their own public access Internet Freenet. But where's the science?

"I volunteered to teach physics there," reports Professor Reichert of the State University of New York at Buffalo. "But this science magnet school has no physics lab. No air table to teach mechanics, no hands-on experiments. All they have is computers."

Schools don't have a duty to provide Internet access. They have a duty to provide an education.

Across the continent, technology in the classroom equates to computers in the classroom. But plenty of other technological devices are essential for teaching, especially in the sciences. "It fries me that we can get cash for computers but we can't buy an optics workbench, a set of voltmeters, or a collection of tuning forks," steams Dr. Reichert. "At a physics teachers meeting, I met a guy who wouldn't pay two thousand dollars for hands-on apparatus to teach magnetic fields and angular momentum. The same guy happily spent twenty times that much on a roomful of computers."

For the cost of two dozen computers, you can equip a terrific high school physics lab. Ten years from now, when those computers are in the trash heap, a set of tuning forks could still teach resonance, a voltmeter could still demonstrate Ohm's law, and students might still learn about angular momentum using that apparatus.

Biology gets snookered by computers, too. Hey—it's much easier to show computer simulations of growing plants, dissected frogs, and crowded ecosystems. Less messy. No offending animal rights activists either. But the effect of replacing biology lab with computational biology is to eviscerate the science and eliminate the sense of exploration and discovery that leads to understanding.

But don't real physicists, chemists, and biologists use computers? Sure. But they didn't learn their professional skills on software. Nor did their schools teach science using simulations. Computer simulations are powerful tools used across the sciences. They yield answers to specific questions. But they don't give understanding, can't demonstrate what it means to do science, won't inspire the curiosity essential to becoming a scientist. They teach simulated science.

There's a bizarre system of grant evaluation that encourages—if not demands—that all new applications have something to do with technology in the classroom. Inevitably, educators apply for computer grants to get money to use elsewhere, say to hire assistants or buy supplies. A screwy way to fund our schools.

Other educators use this money-for-technology fountain as a Trojan mouse. Tell the public that we're bringing computers into the schools; meanwhile sneak in problem-based learning, collaborative learning, or constructivist education. Reformers see technology as a back door through which they'll shake up traditional classrooms. At best, it's an expensive—if disingenuous—way to reform our schools. At worst, it's outright fraud: selling a hidden agenda on the promise that technology will improve our schools.

A waste of teachers' time

There's one area of education where computers have been widely accepted: It's a rare school administrator without a desktop computer. Principals find 'em ideal for tracking attendance, following student grades, making calendars, and writing form letters to parents. As in larger society, educational computing works great at automating administration.

So shouldn't computers reduce school costs by making administrative activities more efficient? I wish it were so. As computers become widely adopted in elementary and high schools, they add a whole new layer of school administrators and middle managers. These include technicians to keep the machines running, content administrators to watch over what the students see, and technology specialists to teach teachers how to best use the digital machines. Save money? Naw.

As schools become networked, I expect teachers' classbooks and attendance rolls to become centralized databases. This won't make the job of teaching any easier, of course. Rather, administrators will gather more information about students (and teachers), generate more paperwork, and further constrain creative teachers. Who'll be happiest? Principals who work in their offices, rather than visiting with teachers, students, and parents. Students who enjoy working alone. Teachers who are more comfortable behind a keyboard than in front of a chalkboard.

But then, teachers may be a disappearing breed. Just as librarians call themselves "information specialists," school systems increasingly hire "information technology professionals" and "technology coordinators." These people search out new ways to use these gizmos, while simultaneously hustling grants for more technostuff.

No surprise, then, to hear that any classroom without a computer is somehow inferior. Peter Hutcher, technology director of the Oakland, California, school district, says, "We have an obligation to provide access to the Internet for students. If they don't have it at home, we darn well better provide it during the school day." Here's Ms. Popp again: "Every day that our children do not have access to the Information Highway is one day less of an excellent education for them."

What nonsense. You certainly can get an excellent education without a computer. And schools don't have a duty to provide Internet access. They have a duty to provide an education.

Is access to television—even children's educational television—necessary to obtain an excellent education? Do schools have an obligation to provide TV to those who don't have it at home?

As much as I love computers, I can't imagine getting an excellent education from any multimedia system. Rather than augmenting the teacher, these machines steal limited class time and direct attention away from scholarship and toward pretty graphics.

Really want to improve classroom teaching? Give teachers more preparation time. Prep time used to be for grading homework and setting up classwork; today, it's increasingly eaten by computers. Each program even the simplest—requires someone to get the computers ready . . . inevitably, it's the teacher. For the dirty secret of educational technology is that computers waste teachers' time, both in and out of the classroom.

No amount of Web searching can make up for a lack of critical thinking or communications skills. No multimedia computer will help a student develop analytic abilities. No microprocessor can augment the creative interplay of hand, clay, and art teacher. No on-line astronomy program can engender the same sense of awe as first seeing the rings of Saturn through a telescope. No computer will encourage a budding athlete to run faster, kick harder, or jump higher.

With or without a computer, a mediocre instructor will never kindle a love for learning. And a good teacher doesn't need the Internet to inspire her students to excellence.

3

Computer-Assisted Education Can Enhance Learning

National Research Council

The National Research Council (NRC) is the research arm of the National Academy of Sciences, a private, nonprofit scholarly society that advises the federal government on scientific and technical matters. The following viewpoint is excerpted from How People Learn: Brain, Mind, Experience, and School, *which summarizes the findings of a two-year project in which the NRC evaluated new developments in the science of learning.*

Computer technology has the potential to dramatically enhance students' educational experience. Computer-assisted education is interactive and therefore captures students' interest better than one-way communications such as lectures or videotapes. Educational software can be used to present both real-world problems and abstract concepts. In addition, tutoring and testing software can be used to analyze students' strengths and weaknesses in a variety of subject areas. The Internet and other networked environments offer students a means for collaborating on projects and a way to interact with the world outside the classroom. Finally, computer-assisted technology can help support teachers' ongoing professional development, which ultimately benefits students.

A ttempts to use computer technologies to enhance learning began with the efforts of pioneers such as R. Atkinson and Patrick Suppes. The presence of computer technology in schools has increased dramatically since that time, and predictions are that this trend will continue to accelerate. The romanticized view of technology is that its mere presence in schools will enhance student learning and achievement. In contrast is the view that money spent on technology, and time spent by students using technology, are money and time wasted. Several groups have reviewed the literature on technology and learning and concluded that it has great potential to enhance student achievement and teacher learning, but only if it is used appropriately.

What is now known about learning provides important guidelines for uses of technology that can help students and teachers develop the competencies needed for the twenty-first century. The new technologies provide opportunities for creating learning environments that extend the possibilities of "old"—but still useful—technologies—books; blackboards; and linear, one-way communication media, such as radio and television shows—as well as offering new possibilities. Technologies do not guarantee effective learning, however. Inappropriate uses of technology can hinder learning—for example, if students spend most of their time picking fonts and colors for multimedia reports instead of planning, writing, and revising their ideas. And everyone knows how much time students can waste surfing the Internet. Yet many aspects of technology make it easier to create environments that fit the principles of learning discussed throughout this report.

Because many new technologies are interactive, it is now easier to create environments in which students can learn by doing, receive feedback, and continually refine their understanding and build new knowledge. The new technologies can also help people visualize difficult-to-understand concepts, such as differentiating heat from temperature. Students can work with visualization and modeling software that is similar to the tools used in nonschool environments, increasing their understanding and the likelihood of transfer from school to nonschool settings. These technologies also provide access to a vast array of information, including digital libraries, data for analysis, and other people who provide information, feedback, and inspiration. They can enhance the learning of teachers and administrators, as well as that of students, and increase connections between schools and the communities, including homes.

In this [viewpoint] we explore how new technologies can be used in five ways:

- bringing exciting curricula based on real-world problems into the classroom;
- providing scaffolds and tools to enhance learning;
- giving students and teachers more opportunities for feedback, reflection, and revision;
- building local and global communities that include teachers, administrators, students, parents, practicing scientists, and other interested people; and
- expanding opportunities for teacher learning.

New curricula

An important use of technology is its capacity to create new opportunities for curriculum and instruction by bringing real-world problems into the classroom for students to explore and solve. Technology can help to create an active environment in which students not only solve problems, but also find their own problems. This approach to learning is very different from the typical school classrooms, in which students spend most of their time learning facts from a lecture or text and doing the problems at the end of the chapter.

Learning through real-world contexts is not a new idea. For a long time, schools have made sporadic efforts to give students concrete experiences through field trips, laboratories, and work-study programs. But these activities have seldom been at the heart of academic instruction, and they have not been easily incorporated into schools because of logistical constraints and the amount of subject material to be covered. Technology offers powerful tools for addressing these constraints, from video-based problems and computer simulations to electronic communications systems that connect classrooms with communities of practitioners in science, mathematics, and other fields.

Because many new technologies are interactive, it is now easier to create environments in which students can learn by doing.

A number of video- and computer-based learning programs are now in use, with many different purposes. The Voyage of the Mimi, developed by Bank Street College, was one of the earliest attempts to use video and computer technology to introduce students to real-life problems: students "go to sea" and solve problems in the context of learning about whales and the Mayan culture of the Yucatan. More recent series include the Jasper Woodbury Problem Solving Series, 12 interactive video environments that present students with challenges that require them to understand and apply important concepts in mathematics. Students who work with the series have shown gains in mathematical problem solving, communication abilities, and attitudes toward mathematics.

New learning programs are not restricted to mathematics and science. Problem-solving environments have also been developed that help students better understand workplaces. For example, in a banking simulation, students assume roles, such as the vice president of a bank, and learn about the knowledge and skills needed to perform various duties.

The interactivity of these technology environments is a very important feature for learning. Interactivity makes it easy for students to revisit specific parts of the environments to explore them more fully, to test ideas, and to receive feedback. Noninteractive environments, like linear videotapes, are much less effective for creating contexts that students can explore and reexamine, both individually and collaboratively.

Another way to bring real-world problems into the classroom is by connecting students with working scientists. In many of these student-scientist partnerships, students collect data that are used to understand global issues; a growing number of them involve students from geographically dispersed schools who interact through the Internet. For example, Global Lab supports an international community of student researchers from more than 200 schools in 30 countries who construct new knowledge about their local and global environments. Global Lab classrooms select aspects of their local environments to study. Using shared tools, curricula, and methodologies, students map, describe, and monitor their sites, collect and share data, and situate their local findings into a broader, global context. After participating in a set of 15 skill-building activities during their first semester, Global Lab students begin advanced research studies in such areas as air and water pollution, background radiation, biodiversity, and ozone depletion. The global perspective helps learners identify environmental phenomena that can be observed around the world, including a decrease in tropospheric ozone levels in places where vegetation is abundant, a dramatic rise of indoor carbon dioxide levels by the end of the school day, and the substantial accumulation of nitrates in certain vegetables. Once participants see significant patterns in their data, this "telecollaborative" community of students, teachers, and scientists tackles the most rigorous aspects of science—designing experiments, conducting peer reviews, and publishing their findings.

Similar approaches have been used in astronomy, ornithology, language arts, and other fields. These collaborative experiences help students understand complex systems and concepts, such as multiple causes and interactions among different variables. Since the ultimate goal of education is to prepare students to become competent adults and lifelong learners, there is a strong argument for electronically linking students not just with their peers, but also with practicing professionals. Increasingly scientists and other professionals are establishing electronic "collaboratories," through which they define and conduct their work. This trend provides both a justification and a medium for establishing virtual communities for learning purposes.

Through Project GLOBE (Global Learning and Observations to Benefit the Environment), thousands of students in grades kindergarten through 12 (K–12) from over 2,000 schools in more than 34 countries are gathering data about their local environments. Students collect data in five different earth science areas, including atmosphere, hydrology, and land cover, using protocols specified by principal investigators from major research institutions. Students submit their data through the Internet to a GLOBE data archive, which both the scientists and the students use to perform their analyses. A set of visualization tools provided on the GLOBE World Wide Web site enables students to see how their own data fit with those collected elsewhere. Students in GLOBE classrooms demonstrate higher knowledge and skill levels on assessments of environmental science methods and data interpretation than their peers who have not participated in the program.

Interactivity makes it easy for students to revisit specific parts of the environments to explore them more fully.

Emerging technologies and new ideas about teaching are being combined to reshape precollege science education in the Learning Through Collaborative Visualization (CoVis) Project. Over wideband networks, middle and high school students from more than 40 schools collaborate with other students at remote locations. Thousands of participating students study atmospheric and environmental sciences—including topics in meteorology and climatology—through project-based activities. Through these networks, students also communicate with "telementors"—university researchers and other experts. Using scientific visualization software, specially modified for learning, students have access to the same research tools and datasets that scientists use.

In one 5-week activity, "Student Conference on Global Warming," supported by curriculum units, learner-centered scientific visualization tools and data, and assessment rubrics available through the CoVis Geo-Sciences web server, students across schools and states evaluate the evidence for global warming and consider possible trends and consequences. Learners are first acquainted with natural variation in climatic temperature, human-caused increases in atmospheric carbon dioxide, and uses of spreadsheets and scientific visualization tools for inquiry. These staging activities specify themes for open-ended collaborative learning projects to follow. In laying out typical questions and data useful to investigate the potential impact of global warming on a country or a country's potential impact on global warming, a general framework is used in which students specialize by selecting a country, its specific data, and the particular issue for their project focus (e.g., rise in carbon-dioxide emissions due to recent growth, deforestation, flooding due to rising sea levels). Students then investigate either a global issue or the point of view of a single country. The results of their investigations are shared in project reports within and across schools, and participants consider current results of international policy in light of their project findings.

Working with practitioners and distant peers on projects with meaning beyond the school classroom is a great motivator for K–12 students. Students are not only enthusiastic about what they are doing, they also produce some impressive intellectual achievements when they can interact with meteorologists, geologists, astronomers, teachers, or computer scientists.

Scaffolds and tools

Many technologies function as scaffolds and tools to help students solve problems. This was foreseen long ago: in a prescient 1945 essay in the *Atlantic Monthly,* Vannevar Bush, science adviser to President Roosevelt, depicted the computer as a general-purpose symbolic system that could serve clerical and other supportive research functions in the sciences, in work, and for learning, thus freeing the human mind to pursue its creative capacities.

In the first generation of computer-based technologies for classroom use, this tool function took the rather elementary form of electronic "flash cards" that students used to practice discrete skills. As applications have spilled over from other sectors of society, computer-based learning tools have become more sophisticated. They now include calculators, spreadsheets, graphing programs, function probes, "mathematical supposers" for making and checking conjectures, and modeling programs for creating and testing models of complex phenomena. In the Middle School Mathematics Through Applications Projects (MMAP), developed at the Institute for Research on Learning, innovative software tools are used for exploring concepts in algebra through such problems as designing insulation for arctic dwellings. In the Little Planet Literacy Series, computer software helps to move students through the phases of becoming better writers. For example, in the Little Planet Literacy Series, engaging video-based adventures encourage kindergarten, first-, and second-grade students to write books to solve challenges posed at the end of the adventures. In one of the challenges, students need to write a book in order to save the creatures on the Little Planet from falling prey to the wiles of an evil character named Wongo.

The challenge for education is to design technologies for learning that draw both from knowledge about human cognition and from practical applications of how technology can facilitate complex tasks in the workplace. These designs use technologies to scaffold thinking and activity, much as training wheels allow young bike riders to practice cycling when they would fall without support. Like training wheels, computer scaffolding enables learners to do more advanced activities and to engage in more advanced thinking and problem solving than they could without such help. Cognitive technologies were first used to help students learn mathematics and writing; a decade later, a multitude of projects use cognitive scaffolds to promote complex thinking, design, and learning in the sciences, mathematics, and writing.

In the Little Planet Literacy Series, computer software helps to move students through the phases of becoming better writers.

The Belvedere system, for example, is designed to teach science-related public policy issues to high school students who lack deep knowledge of many science domains, have difficulty zeroing in on the key issues in a complex scientific debate, and have trouble recognizing abstract relationships that are implicit in scientific theories and arguments. Belvedere uses graphics with specialized boxes to represent different types of relationships among ideas that provide scaffolding to support students' reasoning about science-related issues. As students use boxes and links within Belvedere to represent their understanding of an issue, an on-line adviser gives hints to help them improve the coverage, consistency, and evidence for their arguments.

Scaffolded experiences can be structured in different ways. Some research educators advocate an apprenticeship model, whereby an expert practitioner first models the activity while the learner observes, then scaffolds the learner (with advice and examples), then guides the learner in practice, and gradually tapers off support and guidance until the apprentice can do it alone. Others argue that the goal of enabling a solo approach is unrealistic and overrestrictive since adults often need to use tools or other people to accomplish their work. Some even contend that well-designed technological tools that support complex activities create a truly human-machine symbiosis and may reorganize components of human activity into different structures than they had in pretechnological designs. Although there are varying views on the exact goals and on how to assess the benefits of scaffolding technologies, there is agreement that the new tools make it possible for people to perform and learn in far more complex ways than ever before.

In many fields, experts are using new technologies to represent data in new ways—for example, as three-dimensional virtual models of the surface of Venus or of a molecular structure, either of which can be electronically created and viewed from any angle. Geographical information systems, to take another example, use color scales to visually represent such variables as temperature or rainfall on a map. With these tools, scientists can discern patterns more quickly and detect relationships not previously noticed.

Some scholars assert that simulations and computer-based models are the most powerful resources for the advancement and application of mathematics and science since the origins of mathematical modeling during the Renaissance. The move from a static model in an inert medium, like a drawing, to dynamic models in interactive media that provide visualization and analytic tools is profoundly changing the nature of inquiry in mathematics and science. Students can visualize alternative interpretations as they build models that can be rotated in ways that introduce different perspectives on the problems. These changes affect the kinds of phenomena that can be considered and the nature of argumentation and acceptable evidence.

The same kinds of computer-based visualization and analysis tools that scientists use to detect patterns and understand data are now being adapted for student use. With probes attached to microcomputers, for example, students can do real-time graphing of such variables as acceleration, light, and sound. The ability of the human mind to quickly process and remember visual information suggests that concrete graphics and other visual representations of information can help people learn, as well as help scientists in their work.

A variety of scientific visualization environments for precollege students and teachers have been developed by the CoVis Project. Classrooms can collect and analyze real-time weather data or 25 years of Northern Hemisphere climate data. Or they can investigate the global greenhouse effect. As described above, students with new technological tools can communicate across a network, work with datasets, develop scientific models, and conduct collaborative investigations into meaningful science issues.

> *The same kinds of computer-based visualization and analysis tools that scientists use . . . are now being adapted for student use.*

Since the late 1980s, cognitive scientists, educators, and technologists have suggested that learners might develop a deeper understanding of phenomena in the physical and social worlds if they could build and manipulate models of these phenomena. These speculations are now being tested in classrooms with technology-based modeling tools. For example, the STELLA modeling environment, which grew out of research on systems dynamics at the Massachusetts Institute of Technology, has been widely used for instruction at both the undergraduate and precollege level, in fields as diverse as population ecology and history.

The educational software and exploration and discovery activities developed for the GenScope Project use simulations to teach core topics in genetics as part of precollege biology. The simulations move students through a hierarchy of six key genetic concepts: DNA, cell, chromosome, organism, pedigree, and population. GenScope also uses an innovative hypermodel that allows students to retrieve real-world data to build models of the underlying physical process. Evaluations of the program among high school students in urban Boston found that students not only were enthusiastic about learning this complex subject, but had also made significant conceptual developments.

The Internet is increasingly being used as a forum for students to give feedback to each other.

Students are using interactive computer microworlds to study force and motion in the Newtonian world of mechanics. Through the medium of interactive computer microworlds, learners acquire hands-on and minds-on experience and, thus, a deeper understanding of science. Sixth graders who use computer-based learning tools develop a better conceptual understanding of acceleration and velocity than many 12th-grade physics students. In another project, middle school students employ easy-to-use computer-based tools (Model-It) to build qualitative models of systems, such as the water quality and algae levels in a local stream. Students can insert data they have collected into the model, observe outcomes, and generate what if scenarios to get a better understanding of the interrelationships among key variables.

In general, technology-based tools can enhance student performance when they are integrated into the curriculum and used in accordance with knowledge about learning. But the mere existence of these tools in the classroom provides no guarantee that student learning will improve; they have to be part of a coherent education approach.

Feedback, reflection, and revision

Technology can make it easier for teachers to give students feedback about their thinking and for students to revise their work. Initially, teachers working with the Jasper Woodbury playground adventure (described above) had trouble finding time to give students feedback about their playground designs, but a simple computer interface cut in half the time it took teachers to provide feedback. An interactive Jasper Adventuremaker software program allows students to suggest solutions to a Jasper adventure, then see simulations of the effects of their solutions. The simulations had a clear impact on the quality of the solutions that students generated subsequently. Opportunities to interact with working scientists, as discussed above, also provide rich experiences for learning from feedback and revision. The SMART (Special Multimedia Arenas for Refining Thinking) Challenge Series provides multiple technological resources for feedback and revision. SMART has been tested in various contexts, including the Jasper challenge. When its formative assessment resources are added to these curricula, students achieve at higher levels than without them. . . .

Classroom communication technologies, such as Classtalk, can promote more active learning in large lecture classes and, if used appropriately, highlight the reasoning processes that students use to solve problems. This technology allows an instructor to prepare and display problems that the class works on collaboratively. Students enter answers (individually or as a group) via palm-held input devices, and the technology collects, stores, and displays histograms (bar graphs of how many students preferred each problem solution) of the class responses. This kind of tool can provide useful feedback to students and the teacher on how well the students understand the concepts being covered and whether they can apply them in novel contexts.

Like other technologies, however, Classtalk does not guarantee effective learning. The visual histograms are intended to promote two-way communication in large lecture classes: as a springboard for class discussions in which students justify the procedures they used to arrive at their answers, listen critically to the arguments of others, and refute them or offer other reasoning strategies. But the technology could be used in ways that have nothing to do with this goal. If, for example, a teacher used Classtalk merely as an efficient device to take attendance or administer conventional quizzes, it would not enhance two-way communication or make students' reasoning more visible. With such a use, the opportunity to expose students to varying perspectives on problem solving and the various arguments for different problem solutions would be lost. Thus, effective use of technology involves many teacher decisions and direct forms of teacher involvement.

Modern technologies can help make connections between students' in-school and out-of-school activities.

Peers can serve as excellent sources of feedback. Over the last decade, there have been some very successful and influential demonstrations of how computer networks can support groups of students actively engaged in learning and reflection. Computer-Supported Intentional Learning Environments (CSILE) provide opportunities for students to collaborate on learning activities by working through a communal database that has text and graphics capabilities. Within this networked multimedia environment (now distributed as Knowledge Forum), students create "notes" that contain an idea or piece of information about the topic they are studying. These notes are labeled by categories, such as question or new learning, that other students can search and comment on. With support from the instructor, these processes engage students in dialogues that integrate information and contributions from various sources to produce knowledge. CSILE also includes guidelines for formulating and testing conjectures and prototheories. CSILE has been used in elementary, secondary, and postgraduate classrooms for science, history, and social studies. Students in CSILE classes do better on standardized tests and portfolio entries and show greater depth in their explanations than students in classes without CSILE. Furthermore, students at all ability levels participate effectively: in fact, in classrooms using the technology in the most collaborative fashion, CSILE's positive effects were particularly strong for lower- and middle-ability groups.

As one of its many uses to support learning, the Internet is increasingly being used as a forum for students to give feedback to each other. In the GLOBE Project (described above), students inspect each others' data on the project web site and sometimes find readings they believe may be in error. Students use the electronic messaging system to query the schools that report suspicious data about the circumstances under which they made their measurement; for another kind of use.

As teachers learn to use technology, their own learning has implications for the ways in which they assist students to learn more generally.

An added advantage of networked technologies for communication is that they help make thinking visible. This core feature of the cognitive apprenticeship model of instruction is exemplified in a broad range of instructional programs and has a technological manifestation, as well. By prompting learners to articulate the steps taken during their thinking processes, the software creates a record of thought that learners can use to reflect on their work and teachers can use to assess student progress. Several projects expressly include software designed to make learners' thinking visible. In CSILE, for example, as students develop their communal hypermedia database with text and graphics, teachers can use the database as a record of students' thoughts and electronic conversations over time. Teachers can browse the database to review both their students' emerging understanding of key concepts and their interaction skills.

The CoVis Project developed a networked hypermedia database, the collaboratory notebook, for a similar purpose. The collaboratory notebook is divided into electronic workspaces, called notebooks, that can be used by students working together on a specific investigation. The notebook provides options for making different kinds of pages—questions, conjectures, evidence for, evidence against, plans, steps in plans, information, and commentary. Using the hypermedia system, students can pose a question, then link it to competing conjectures about the questions posed by different students (perhaps from different sites) and to a plan for investigating the question. Images and documents can be electronically "attached" to pages. Using the notebook shortened the time between students' preparation of their laboratory notes and the receipt of feedback from their teachers. Similar functions are provided by Speak-Easy, a software tool used to structure and support dialogues among engineering students and their instructors.

Computer-based tutoring environments

Sophisticated tutoring environments that pose problems are also now available and give students feedback on the basis of how experts reason and organize their knowledge in physics, chemistry, algebra, computer programming, history, and economics. With this increased understanding has come an interest in: testing theories of expert reasoning by translating them into computer programs, and using computer-based expert systems as part of a larger program to teach novices. Combining an expert model with a student model—the system's representation of the student's level of knowledge—and a pedagogical model that drives the system has produced intelligent tutoring systems, which seek to combine the advantages of customized one-on-one tutoring with insights from cognitive research about expert performance, learning processes, and naive reasoning.

A variety of computer-based cognitive tutors have been developed for algebra, geometry, and LISP programming. These cognitive tutors have resulted in a complex profile of achievement gains for the students, depending on the nature of the tutor and the way it is integrated into the classroom.

Another example of the tutoring approach is the Sherlock Project, a computer-based environment for teaching electronics troubleshooting to Air Force technicians who work on a complex system involving thousands of parts. A simulation of this complex system was combined with an expert system or coach that offered advice when learners reached impasses in their troubleshooting attempts; and with reflection tools that allowed users to replay their performance and try out possible improvements. In several field tests of technicians as they performed the hardest real-world troubleshooting tasks, 20 to 25 hours of Sherlock training was the equivalent of about 4 years of on-the-job experience. Not surprisingly, Sherlock has been deployed at several U.S. Air Force bases. Two of the crucial properties of Sherlock are modeled on successful informal learning: learners successfully complete every problem they start, with the amount of coaching decreasing as their skill increases; and learners replay and reflect on their performance, highlighting areas where they could improve, much as a football player might review a game film.

It is noteworthy that students can use these tutors in groups as well as alone. In many settings, students work together on tutors and discuss issues and possible answers with others in their class.

Connecting classrooms to community

It is easy to forget that student achievement in school also depends on what happens outside of school. Bringing students and teachers in contact with the broader community can enhance their learning. . . . Universities and businesses, for example, have helped communities upgrade the quality of teaching in schools. Engineers and scientists who work in industry often play a mentoring role with teachers.

Modern technologies can help make connections between students' in-school and out-of-school activities. For example, the "transparent school" uses telephones and answering machines to help parents understand the daily assignments in classrooms. Teachers need only a few minutes per day to dictate assignments into an answering machine. Parents can call at their convenience and retrieve the daily assignments, thus becoming informed of what their children are doing in school. Contrary to some expectations, low-income parents are as likely to call the answering machines as are parents of higher socioeconomic status.

The Internet can also help link parents with their children's schools. School calendars, assignments, and other types of information can be posted on a school's Internet site. School sites can also be used to inform the community of what a school is doing and how they can help. For example, the American Schools Directory (www.asd.com), which has created Internet pages for each of the 106,000 public and private K–12 schools in the country, includes a "Wish List" on which schools post requests for various kinds of help. In addition, the ASD provides free e-mail for every student and teacher in the country.

Computer-based technologies hold great promise . . .
as a means of promoting learning.

Several projects are exploring the factors required to create effective electronic communities. For example, we noted above that students can learn more when they are able to interact with working scientists, authors, and other practicing professionals. An early review of six different electronic communities, which included teacher and student networks and a group of university researchers, looked at how successful these communities were in relation to their size and location, how they organized themselves, what opportunities and obligations for response were built into the network, and how they evaluated their work. Across the six groups, three factors were associated with successful network-based communities: an emphasis on group rather than one-to-one communication; well-articulated goals or tasks; and explicit efforts to facilitate group interaction and establish new social norms.

To make the most of the opportunities for conversation and learning available through these kinds of networks, students, teachers, and mentors must be willing to assume new or untraditional roles. For example, a major purpose of the Kids as Global Scientists (KGS) research project—a worldwide cluster of students, scientist mentors, technology experts, and experts in pedagogy—is to identify key components that make these communities successful. In the most effective interactions, a social glue develops between partners over time. Initially, the project builds relationships by engaging people across locations in organized dialogues and multimedia introductions; later, the group establishes guidelines and scaffolds activities to help all participants understand their new responsibilities. Students pose questions about weather and other natural phenomena and refine and respond to questions posed by themselves and others. This dialogue-based approach to learning creates a rich intellectual context, with ample opportunities for participants to improve their understanding and become more personally involved in explaining scientific phenomena.

Teacher learning

The introduction of new technologies to classrooms has offered new insights about the roles of teachers in promoting learning. Technology can give teachers license to experiment and tinker. It can stimulate teachers to think about the processes of learning, whether through a fresh study of their own subject or a fresh perspective on students' learning. It softens the barrier between what students do and what teachers do.

When teachers learn to use a new technology in their classrooms, they model the learning process for students; at the same time, they gain new insights on teaching by watching their students learn. Moreover, the transfer of the teaching role from teacher to student often occurs spontaneously during efforts to use computers in classrooms. Some children develop a profound involvement with some aspect of the technology or the software, spend considerable time on it, and know more than anyone else in the group, including their teachers. Often both teachers and students are novices, and the creation of knowledge is a genuinely cooperative endeavor. Epistemological authority—teachers possessing knowledge and students receiving knowledge—is redefined, which in turn redefines social authority and personal responsibility. Cooperation creates a setting in which novices can contribute what they are able and learn from the contributions of those more expert than they. Collaboratively, the group, with its variety of expertise, engagement, and goals, gets the job done. This devolution of authority and move toward cooperative participation results directly from, and contributes to, an intense cognitive motivation.

As teachers learn to use technology, their own learning has implications for the ways in which they assist students to learn more generally:

- They must be partners in innovation; a critical partnership is needed among teachers, administrators, students, parents, community, university, and the computer industry.
- They need time to learn: time to reflect, absorb discoveries, and adapt practices.
- They need collegial advisers rather than supervisors; advising is a partnership.

Internet-based communities of teachers are becoming an increasingly important tool for overcoming teachers' sense of isolation. They also provide avenues for geographically dispersed teachers who are participating in the same kinds of innovations to exchange information and offer support to each other. Examples of these communities include the LabNet Project, which involves over 1,000 physics teachers; Bank Street College's Mathematics Learning project; the QUILL network for Alaskan teachers of writing; and the HumBio Project, in which teachers are developing biology curricula over the network. WEBCSILE, an Internet version of the CSILE program described above, is being used to help create teacher communities.

The World Wide Web provides another venue for teachers to communicate with an audience outside their own institutions. At the University of Illinois, James Levin asks his education graduate students to develop web pages with their evaluations of education resources on the web, along with hot links to those web resources they consider most valuable. Many students not only put up these web pages, but also revise and maintain them after the course is over. Some receive tens of thousands of hits on their web sites each month.

While e-mail, listservs, and web sites have enabled members of teacher communities to exchange information and to stay in touch, they represent only part of technology's full potential to support real communities of practice. Teacher communities of practice need chances for planned interactions, tools for joint review and annotation of education resources, and opportunities for on-line collaborative design activities. In general, teacher communities need environments that generate the social glue that Songer found so important in the Kids as Global Scientists community.

The Teacher Professional Development Institute (TAPPED IN), a multiuser virtual environment, integrates synchronous ("live") and asynchronous (such as e-mail) communication. Users can store and share documents and interact with virtual objects in an electronic environment patterned after a typical conference center. Teachers can log into TAPPED IN to discuss issues, create and share resources, hold workshops, engage in mentoring, and conduct collaborative inquiries with the help of virtual versions of such familiar tools as books, whiteboards, file cabinets, notepads, and bulletin boards. Teachers can wander among the public "rooms," exploring the resources in each and engaging in spontaneous live conversations with others exploring the same resources. More than a dozen major teacher professional development organizations have set up facilities within TAPPED IN.

The introduction of new technologies to classrooms has offered new insights about the roles of teachers in promoting learning.

In addition to supporting teachers' ongoing communication and professional development, technology is used in preservice seminars for teachers. A challenge in providing professional development for new teachers is allowing them adequate time to observe accomplished teachers and to try their own wings in classrooms, where innumerable decisions must be made in the course of the day and opportunities for reflection are few. Prospective teachers generally have limited exposure to classrooms before they begin student teaching, and teacher trainers tend to have limited time to spend in classes with them, observing and critiquing their work. Technology can help overcome these constraints by capturing the complexity of classroom interactions in multiple media. For example, student teachers can replay videos of classroom events to learn to read subtle classroom clues and see important features that escaped them on first viewing.

Databases have been established to assist teachers in a number of subject areas. One is a video archive of mathematics lessons from third- and fifth-grade classes, taught by experts Magdalene Lampert and Deborah Ball. The lessons model inquiry-oriented teaching, with students working to solve problems and reason and engaging in lively discussions about the mathematics underlying their solutions. The videotapes allow student teachers to stop at any point in the action and discuss nuances of teacher performance with their fellow students and instructors. Teachers' annotations and an archive of student work associated with the lessons further enrich the resource.

A multimedia database of video clips of expert teachers using a range of instructional and classroom management strategies has been established by Indiana University and the North Central Regional Educational Laboratory. Each lesson comes with such materials as the teacher's lesson plan, commentary by outside experts, and related research articles. Another technological resource is a set of video-based cases (on videodisc and CD-ROM) for teaching reading that shows prospective teachers a variety of different approaches to reading instruction. The program also includes information about the school and community setting, the philosophy of the school principals, a glimpse of what the teachers did before school started, and records of the students' work as they progress throughout the year.

A different approach is shown in interactive multimedia databases illustrating mathematics and science teaching, developed at Vanderbilt University. Two of the segments, for example, provide edited video tapes of the same teacher teaching two second-grade science lessons. In one lesson, the teacher and students discuss concepts of insulation presented in a textbook chapter; in the second lesson, the teacher leads the students in a hands-on investigation of the amount of insulation provided by cups made of different materials. On the surface, the teacher appears enthusiastic and articulate in both lessons and the students are well behaved. Repeated viewings of the tapes, however, reveal that the students' ability to repeat the correct words in the first lesson may mask some enduring misconceptions. The misconceptions are much more obvious in the context of the second lesson.

In yet a different way in which technology can support preservice teacher preparation, education majors enrolled at the University of Illinois who were enrolled in lower division science courses like biology were electronically linked up to K–12 classrooms to answer student questions about the subject area. The undergraduates helped the K–12 students explore the science. More important, the education majors had a window into the kinds of questions that elementary or high school students ask in the subject domain, thus motivating them to get more out of their university science courses.

The promise of computer-assisted education

Technology has become an important instrument in education. Computer-based technologies hold great promise both for increasing access to knowledge and as a means of promoting learning. The public imagination has been captured by the capacity of information technologies to centralize and organize large bodies of knowledge; people are excited by the prospect of information networks, such as the Internet, linking students around the globe into communities of learners.

What has not yet been fully understood is that computer-based technologies can be powerful pedagogical tools—not just rich sources of information, but also extensions of human capabilities and contexts for social interactions supporting learning. The process of using technology to improve learning is never solely a technical matter, concerned only with properties of educational hardware and software. Like a textbook or any other cultural object, technology resources for education—whether a software science simulation or an interactive reading exercise—function in a social environment, mediated by learning conversations with peers and teachers.

4

Computer-Assisted Education May Not Enhance Learning

Alison Armstrong and Charles Casement

Alison Armstrong and Charles Casement are coauthors of The Child and the Machine: How Computers Put Our Children's Education at Risk, *from which the following viewpoint was excerpted.*

The idea that computers in the classroom enhance learning is so widely accepted that few people have questioned it. In reality, there is little evidence to show that computer-assisted education improves students' academic achievement. Research on the subject is ambiguous, and much of it is flawed because it uses standardized testing, which provides a very narrow measure of student achievement. Some research suggests that too much computer use can actually harm students' academic performance, and other studies show that computers in the classroom cause teachers to spend less time with students.

Parents naturally want the best possible education for their children. Just as the parents of baby boomers purchased home encyclopedias in record numbers, today's parents are buying computers and software to give their children what they believe to be a head start in their education. But whereas parents in the past might have waited until their children could read before purchasing home encyclopedias, today's parents are buying computers and software (known as lap ware) for their preschoolers, including babies as young as eight months old. Hoping to provide children with an advantage before formal schooling begins, parents are turning their toddlers into a generation of cybertots.

Like the encyclopedia salesmen, software marketing companies are targeting families with young children, and the market for home computers and learning software is growing even faster than the school market. In 1995, approximately 30 percent of U.S. homes had a personal computer. By 1999, this figure had risen to more than 50 percent. Parents want their children to have this magical tool whose use has become synonymous with academic success and marketable skills. They fear that without this vital piece of technology, their children will be left behind, ending up intellectually undernourished and almost certainly unemployed.

The exaggerated promises of computer advertising

Public perception of the computer as a passport to success has been heightened by the industry's relentless advertising. Advertisements designed to humanize the technology give computers friendly personalities and a desire to please. "You won't believe the things I do for this family," says an AST computer, which then describes how it helps "Junior," "Ms. Social Success," Mom, and Dad.

In another glossy magazine, a child cozied up with a computer is pronounced "the head of the class"—a favorite slogan in Apple's promotion of its technology. Apple and Microsoft also use television regularly to advertise the virtues and advantages of home computing, although the scenarios presented are sometimes less than convincing. One Apple commercial shows a father and his young son apparently bonding while looking at the computer screen. At one point, the father smiles proudly and caresses the back of his son's head. Oblivious to his father's touch, the child is totally absorbed in the screen.

Behind the comforting assurance that computers are part of a close-knit family life is another, more urgent theme—children need computers because those who have them will outperform those who do not. At least, this is the assumption behind a number of computer hardware and software advertisements. Take, for example, a double-page advertisement for Microsoft's *Encarta* multimedia encyclopedia that appeared several years ago. "Forget Goldilocks and the Three Bears, tell us about Sartre," the headline reads. The ad continues: "'C'mon, dad, tell us about Sartre and existentialism and his belief in the inescapable responsibility of all individuals for their own decisions and his relationship with Simone de Beauvoir,' we pleaded as he tucked us in for the night." The ad shows the faces of two little girls who cannot be more than six years old.

Even less convincing is a Sears Brand Central ad showing a little girl standing behind a computer with her arms stretched above her head. "She may be only 5 but she's light-years ahead. By the time she reaches first grade, she'll have *traveled* to Jupiter and back." The computer monitor shows two planets in false proximity to each other. What help "traveling" to Jupiter will be to a first grader is left unexplained.

The message conveyed by this advertising onslaught is that children with computers will outperform those without them. But do computers really enhance learning? Does consistent and convincing evidence exist to support this view?

What the research shows

Educators have been conducting research into the link between computers and improved academic performance for more than thirty years. In the past two decades, thousands of studies have been conducted in classrooms across the United States in an attempt to examine the effectiveness of computer-based instruction.

The evidence that emerges is inconclusive at best. Reviews of research published between 1985 and 1998 show mixed and sometimes contradictory results. For example, researchers at the Center for Research on Learning and Teaching at the University of Michigan analyzed the results of 254 controlled evaluation studies and concluded that computer-based instruction "usually produces positive effects on students." Specifically, their analysis showed that the average student in a class receiving computer-based instruction would outperform 62 percent of students in a class not using computers. On the other hand, a research team from Florida A&M University and Florida State University found a number of reviews that showed no significant difference in performance between students who were using computers and those who were not.

Results of several individual large-scale projects also do little to provide support for computer-based instruction. For example, the Minnesota Technology Demonstration Project, undertaken in the mid-1980s, involved more than 20 percent of the state's school districts. Researchers who studied computer-using fourth, fifth, and sixth graders over a two-year period discovered that, on average, these students did not perform as well in math, reading, and language arts as students taught by traditional methods.

Results of several individual large-scale projects . . . do little to provide support for computer-based instruction.

Educators and parents must realize, too, that where the results were positive, not all students benefited equally. Generally, boys appeared to perform better than girls, and low-achieving students showed more improvement than average students.

Studies looking at the effects of integrated learning systems (ILSs) show similar, unconvincing, or at best, problematic results. In an ILS, a central management system links individual computers that are placed either in a computer lab or in the library, or distributed among classrooms throughout the school. The system delivers courses as part of a school's standard curriculum. The subjects most commonly taught by this method are math, reading, and language arts. Students may spend thirty minutes a week or more working on practice drills presented on their computer screens, which are really just electronic workbooks. Newer applications have graphics and sound.

A frequently cited advantage of ILSs is that students work at their own pace. The system determines the level each student has reached in each subject and presents the lesson accordingly. The computer provides immediate feedback to the student and records the work. By monitoring the results, teachers are able to assess where their students are having difficulty and provide the necessary assistance.

At best, however, these systems have been only moderately successful in raising students' academic achievement. In some cases their effectiveness has simply been exaggerated. In an extensive review of ILS evaluation reports, Henry Jay Becker of the University of California at Irvine suggests that some studies (including the most widely cited) substantially overreport the effectiveness of ILSs. As well, only lower- and higher-achieving students appeared to benefit from using this technology. Students in the middle range (the majority) performed better when taught by their teachers.

Becker also cautions that evaluating the results of ILS programs is difficult because of the quality of the research. In a majority of studies, for example, poor evaluation design (which includes failure to compare students' performance with that of a control group receiving traditional instruction) is compounded by inadequate data collection, poor data analysis, inadequate description of how the program operated and the conditions in which it was used, or a combination of these.

One reason why ILSs do not achieve more impressive results is that they promote individualized problem solving at the expense of interaction with peers. Childhood learning is primarily a social activity, however, and children learn as much, if not more, through talking with their teachers and other students as they do by solving problems on their own. Where an ILS is in place, children have fewer opportunities for discussion not only with other children, but also with their teachers. Given that self-paced instruction is possible with an ILS, each child could conceivably work at a different rate on a different program. This means that little context would exist in which children could discuss their classroom work, and they would have fewer opportunities to share problem-solving strategies. Such systems make it difficult for teachers to focus class lessons and discussions.

Critic Douglas Noble views the growth in the use of ILS programs as a potential catastrophe. He believes that increased use of such systems "will almost certainly lead to more reliance on standardized testing to measure achievement," something for which an ILS is ideally suited. There will thus be a tendency "to reduce education to skills and facts preprogrammed into the computer, leaving little role for reflection, imagination, discovery, and creativity." This creates a kind of educational straitjacket in which "children are viewed as 'things' that are taught to perform specified tasks rather than as human beings to be cultivated." The fact that ILS programs appear to be effective only if used intensively seems to bear out his concerns.

With a growing pressure for accountability, the computer seems, at first glance, an ideal means of objectively measuring student achievement. It appears to be the perfect equalizer—one which does not play favorites. Yet not only does computer technology work better for some students than for others, but it also cannot accommodate the wide variety of learning styles evident in any classroom.

Problems with the research

Even where the use of computers appears to improve academic performance, we must approach the results with caution. First, most research studies take place over a relatively short period, often no more than three months. It is difficult to determine whether gains made in such a short time indicate a long-term trend or whether they merely reflect students' increased interest and motivation as a result of the attention lavished on them by the researchers and the novelty of using computers. When the novelty wears off, students' interest and performance may well return to previous levels.

In addition, the type of work that students do on computers is still mainly drill and practice and is not likely to interest them once the initial thrill of using a computer has dissipated. In spite of games and appealing graphics, once using a computer becomes routine, students find that they have no real control over what they are doing, and learning becomes dull and repetitive.

Not only does computer technology work better for some students than for others, but it also cannot accommodate the wide variety of learning styles evident in any classroom.

A Tennessee study discovered that students' attitudes toward computers changed the more they used them. Over a three-year period, students' enjoyment of the technology declined steadily, confirming that the novelty of using any technology plays a significant role in learning. In addition, the older students were generally less enthusiastic about computers than younger students, and the girls' responses were consistently more negative than the boys'.

The novelty effect is one reason why so many people believe that computers can motivate students and thereby improve their academic performance—motivation is a critical factor in determining how well children perform in school. The intensity with which children play video games makes many parents think that such enthusiasm will spill over into math, language, or science activities.

There is no proof, however, that such enthusiasm translates to other areas of learning. In a study involving six schools and 803 first and second graders, researchers at the Tokyo Institute of Technology studied the effectiveness of using computers to enhance creativity and motivation in primary school children. They found that the children who used computers appeared to have a more positive attitude toward the technology— a finding consistent with a number of North American studies. Computer use did not, however, encourage greater creativity or motivate the children to study more. What *did* motivate them were creative experiences such as reading books and saying rhymes.

In addition to the novelty effect, there is another reason for having reservations about the results of research studies; this concerns the role of teachers in implementing these studies. Students in experimental groups (those using computers) and those in control groups (not using computers) are often taught by different teachers, so that it is impossible to determine whether the teacher made the difference rather than the technology itself. If teachers enjoy working with computers and believe in their value as a learning tool, their enthusiasm is more likely to transfer to their students, at least in the short term.

Although some teachers get excited about using new computer-based materials and approaches, other ways of giving them fresh challenges certainly exist. Some schools, for instance, have discovered that when teachers attend workshops in the creative arts, their motivation and enthusiasm improve significantly. Computer technology is not the only way to reinvigorate a tired curriculum and listless students.

So why has there not been more public debate about the limitations of computer-based instruction? This is due, in part, to the selective nature of the information that is reported. Positive results receive more attention and are more likely to be published than negative ones. Companies that produce and market educational computer programs conduct and publicize the results of their own studies, which tend to place their products in a favorable light. Discussion of research studies that are critical of computer-based instruction has only recently made its way into the mainstream media. The belief that computer technology will positively influence our childen's education is so widely held that few have questioned it.

> *The belief that computer technology will positively influence our children's education is so widely held that few have questioned it.*

Separating advertising copy from journalism is often difficult. Don Tapscott, author of *Growing Up Digital: The Rise of the Net Generation,* wrote:

> interactive software makes learning more fun for many children. . . . Early research indicates that the technology holds great promise—children appear to learn the three Rs more quickly and are more motivated to explore new subjects.

A recent television commercial for Patriot computers shows a pretty blonde teacher in an elementary school classroom demonstrating the latest software while proclaiming computers

> make learning fun as our kids perfect their reading, writing, and math skills. They can delve into the worlds of science, history, and geography, using interactive technology. . . .
> Ask yourself this: Do you want the best for your children?

Critical writing on the subject of computer technology began to emerge only in the past few years. One notable exception to the trend of media bias came from the *San Jose Mercury News,* a daily newspaper based in the heart of Silicon Valley. In 1995, the paper, led by journalist Christopher Schmitt, examined the link between academic achievement and computer technology to discover whether schools that had significant relationships with technology outperformed those that used computers to a lesser extent. In other words, was computer technology a significant factor in improving students' academic achievement?

The study examined the results of a 1994 statewide test, the California Learning Assessment Study (CLAS), in reading, writing, and mathematics. Taking each school's average in these subject areas, researchers tried to find a link between schools with high technology use and those with high averages.

The *Mercury News* did not find in favor of the technology:

> In general, the analysis showed no strong link between the

presence of technology—or the use of technology in teaching—and superior achievement. The only exception was found in schools serving low-income students, where there was a stronger association between achievement and technology investment.

The significance of the *Mercury News* study, however, lies not just in its results, but also in the type of test that produced them. Despite being controversial (it has since been discontinued for political reasons), the CLAS was regarded as an improvement over other standardized tests in that it attempted to measure the quality of students' thinking and their achievement across the curriculum, rather than their ability merely to memorize facts, fill in the blanks, or select the correct answers to multiple-choice questions. By using the CLAS, the *Mercury News* study had at its core a much broader assessment of students' abilities than is normally used in studies that evaluate the effects of computer-based instruction.

Potential harms of computer-based education

More recent research in this field suggests that too much computer use in class can actually hurt students' academic performance. A study undertaken by the New Jersey–based Educational Testing Service (ETS), which examined data from the 1996 National Assessment of Educational Progress (NAEP) in mathematics, found that frequent computer use in school tended to have a negative effect on the math scores of fourth and eighth graders. Students did not benefit from using computers more often, but from using them in particular ways.

For example, eighth-grade students who learned higher-order thinking skills through computer simulations—which allow students to examine the concept of velocity, for instance—had higher math scores than students who used drill-and-practice programs, which focus on lower-order thinking skills. Children can only benefit from such higher-level uses of technology, however, when they are developmentally ready to do so, and when their teachers are adequately trained.

Among fourth-grade students, frequent computer use at home had a negative impact on math scores. The opposite was true for eighth-grade students. This may be because older students were not playing video games or using low-level software at home; instead, they were using computers for word processing and research.

Black and low-income students had less access to home computers than white students and those from higher-income families. But the real inequality lay not with computer access, but with how well trained the teachers were in technology and how computers were used in class. Most troubling, said the study's author, Harold Wenglinsky, was the fact that black (and poor) children tend to use computers to learn basic arithmetic more often than white (and wealthier) children and that the programs they use are mainly for low-level exercises such as drill-and-practice programs. Their teachers are also less likely to have received training in the use of technology.

Inexperienced teachers who rely on computers in the elementary school years may be unwittingly abandoning their students because the makers of many software packages stress the fact that these will "free the teacher" to work with other students. This means that when students are occupied with the technology, they often receive little or no attention from their teacher.

Educational researchers Larry Miller and J. Dale Burnett have cast some light on this issue, suggesting that sometimes inexperienced teachers simply "set it and forget it," meaning that they set up students at a computer and then leave them to work alone. Not only do students sometimes miss out on enriching group activities such as story reading or discussion because they are preoccupied with the computer, but they also miss out on interaction with their teachers. "This observation was especially interesting," say Miller and Burnett,

> because it was different from their normal behavior where interactions with students were frequent. For example, when students engaged in seat work, these teachers would move from child to child, asking questions, clarifying problems, reteaching when necessary, and offering encouragement.

One teacher simply said, "The computer program is looking after their needs, and, besides, I get a printout of their performance."

The ETS study concludes that middle school students in grades seven and eight are more likely to benefit from using computer technology than children in elementary schools. This makes sense because regardless of how sophisticated the software program, it is simply no substitute for a teacher when a child needs answers to complex questions. As children grow older, they are more able to work independently and, because they now possess some basic skills, may derive greater benefits from using the computer for more sophisticated learning. Significantly, the ETS study found that private school students used computers less frequently than public school students in the fourth grade, but more frequently in the eighth grade.

It is difficult, if not impossible, to measure accurately the impact of computers on learning. This is not only because it is virtually impossible to separate the role of the technology versus that of the teacher, but also because of the nature of the achievement tests themselves.

The drawbacks of standardized testing

There are, in fact, well-documented limitations of the standardized tests that are generally used to assess the effects of computer-based instruction. The rationale of standardized tests is that they measure students' ability to perform well in school. But, to a large extent, the scores *determine* how well they will perform in school. What a test does is measure how well students are likely to do on subsequent tests of a similar nature. High test scores are not related to the depth or scope of students' learning, but merely to their test-taking abilities.

The origins of standardized testing go back to Sir Francis Galton, a cousin of Charles Darwin and creator of the infamous bell curve. In 1869, Galton published *Hereditary Genius,* a book in which he hypothesized that one could measure the degree to which people differed from one another in intelligence. He devised a way of representing the distribution of intelligence among a given population by constructing a curve, based on a purely imaginary scale, which showed that 50 percent of individuals would fall within the middle (normal) range, and the remainder would be divided equally among those of lesser or greater intelligence. The resulting curve was in the shape of a bell.

Galton assumed, then, that intelligence could be measured on a linear scale and that such measurement would result in a bell-curve distribution. These assumptions were based on no scientific proof whatsoever.

There are . . . well-documented limitations of the standardized tests that are generally used to assess the effects of computer-based instruction.

It is important to understand that standardized tests are designed to produce scores that conform to the bell curve. In other words, their level of difficulty is calibrated to ensure that half the students score above the norm and half below. Rather than assessing students fairly on skills and knowledge they might reasonably be expected to possess, the tests are constructed to create, as Herbert Kohl put it, "a hierarchy of success or failure." This is done in the name of an untested hypothesis that is supported by a completely arbitrary measurement of intelligence, a concept that, in many respects, still defies definition.

A standardized test provides a very narrow measure of a person's capabilities. Harvard University psychologist Howard Gardner has suggested that everyone possesses a number of intelligences, which contribute in varying degrees to each person's potential. In his book *Frames of Mind: The Theory of Multiple Intelligences,* Gardner differentiated among seven kinds of intelligence: logical–mathematical, linguistic, musical, spatial, bodily–kinesthetic, interpersonal, and intrapersonal.

For example, writers are more likely to be strong in linguistic intelligence, athletes in bodily–kinesthetic intelligence, and visual artists and chess players in spatial intelligence. The traditional straight-A student demonstrates a high degree of logical–mathematical intelligence—the type of intelligence measured predominantly by standardized tests. By focusing on one type of intelligence, such tests ignore other forms of intelligence that can promote success later in life and, as a result, often fail to predict how well a child will do at the postsecondary school level or in the workplace. The fact that high test scores cannot necessarily be equated with later achievement lends support to the view that intelligence is multifaceted and cannot be measured by means of a simple test with "right" and "wrong" answers. Although current modes of intelligence testing appear to offer numerical precision, they are often conceptually flawed.

Just as disturbing is the fact that generations of researchers have discovered that standardized testing results in a narrowing of the curriculum. Where these tests are administered, teachers, and indeed whole school districts, begin to alter their curriculum in order to ensure that their students score high on the tests. But the teach-to-the-test approach has proven unwise. In such situations, students soon learn to be good test takers, but perhaps little else. As many critics have suggested, improved test scores do not necessarily mean that students are learning more. They may, in fact, be learning less. As teacher and writer William Hynes has said, "What produces good exam-taker is the opposite of what produces a citizen of literate habits."

In addition, most tests do not measure students' ability to analyze and solve problems and apply their skills and knowledge in other contexts. Indeed, without direct teacher involvement and evaluation, thinking skills are difficult both to teach and measure.

Software developers often claim that computer use in classrooms gives teachers more opportunities to be involved with their students on an individual basis, but direct teacher involvement can be better achieved by reducing class sizes rather than by putting children in front of computers. Smaller class sizes have a positive impact on children's academic performance. This is especially true of young children.

The 1984–1990 Student/Teacher Achievement Ratio (STAR) Project study out of Tennessee provides striking evidence. The study, involving more than 7,000 children, found that smaller class sizes allowed students more contact with their teacher and resulted in strong academic and social gains. Students also achieved consistently higher scores in their statewide tests. In fact, these gains continued throughout high school. Teachers reported a greater awareness of their students' family lives and had fewer discipline problems. Because teachers were able to give children more individual attention, they could identify children who had learning disabilities or who were having trouble with reading or arithmetic earlier, and these children received remedial instruction. And with fewer students in the classroom, teachers suffered less fatigue.

Our schools spend vast sums of money on the integration of technology, the effects of which are often counterproductive.

The cost to Tennessee, a traditionally poor state, was $1 billion. But the parents, teachers, and school administration believe the money is well spent. In 1988, elementary class sizes were cut virtually in half, and in 1989 the state legislated a fifteen-student cap on class sizes. Now seventeen other states have begun to follow Tennessee's lead. California, for example, launched a program to trim class sizes in the first through fourth grades, and in spite of difficulties in obtaining certified teachers and sufficient classroom space, teachers report high levels of satisfaction with the program. Perhaps if more school districts cut class sizes (and certainly this is a direction that early-childhood educators have urged for decades), school districts would have less reason to spend money on technology and more reason to focus on the relationship between student and teacher. Reducing class size also has another advantage: all students benefit equally.

Although the initial costs of reducing class sizes are high, school districts can find cost savings in other areas. Children who fail a grade in elementary school must repeat the grade, which costs the school system as well as the child. When class sizes are kept small, teachers can more quickly identify learning problems that are often undiagnosed in larger classes. When the system fails to identify a child with special needs when he or she is young, these problems become more difficult—and often more expensive—to fix later.

Learning out of context

One of the biggest problems with educational software that is designed to improve test scores is that it takes learning out of context. But children need a meaningful context for learning so that they can make connections between abstract knowledge and concrete experience. When children use educational software to enhance their factual knowledge, they are expected to answer questions or solve problems with no other point of reference.

We find scant evidence that using such software results in smarter or more enthusiastic students. For example, a California study of fifth and sixth graders compared those who played *Where in the World Is Carmen Sandiego?* with students who drew maps and played noncomputer games involving the same geography facts. It found no significant differences between the groups in either their ability to recall facts or their attitudes toward the study of geography.

Where in the World Is Carmen Sandiego? is by far the best-selling educational software in North America. The game first appeared in the mid-1980s and has been followed by six sequels, three of which are also among the top five best-sellers. These programs use a detective game to teach geography and history. According to one review, teachers like the *Carmen* games because they send students scurrying to look up facts in reference books. (In the original versions of *Carmen Sandiego*, these consisted of *Fodor's USA Travel Guide* and *The World Almanac and Book of Facts*; later versions enable students to conduct searches on CD–ROM.) "The software," writes a *Home PC* reviewer,

> gives children a context for the geographical and historical information they uncover, so they tend to understand and retain it. . . . The idea is to keep children from being passive learners.

Thoughtful teachers, however, might have reservations about using a format that arbitrarily jumps all over the place, preferring, instead, an approach that allows children to explore a single topic from various angles and gives them time to absorb and fit together the details of what they are learning. While playing one of the *Carmen* sequels, *Where in Time Is Carmen Sandiego?*, we discovered that the game propelled us around the world on a whirlwind tour that never stopped long enough in any one place to show what was really going on. For example, during the game the following facts appeared on the screen, in this order:

- The founders of the unified Russian State were ruthless in the pursuit of their goals. Ivan the Terrible was notorious for the cruelty of his methods.
- Commercial dynasties such as the Medici family of Florence controlled much of the wealth and power in Renaissance Italy.
- Francisco Pizarro, a Spanish conquistador, sailed to Peru in the mid-

1500s. There he ambushed the Incan ruler and forced him to pay a ransom of a room full of gold.

• Holland in the fifteenth and sixteenth centuries was first ruled by France and then by Spain. The Eighty Years' War ended Spanish rule and ushered in Dutch independence.

Such information is skimpy and sometimes misleading. On the last two items, minimal research revealed the following: Pizarro in fact made two voyages to Peru, the first in 1526 and the second, his voyage of conquest, in 1531, and the unnamed Incan ruler was Atahualpa; and the Eighty Years' War in fact ended in 1648, in the mid-seventeenth century. This kind of whistle-stop info-tour is of questionable educational value because the purpose of looking up information is to solve clues to Carmen's whereabouts rather than learn more about the times and places involved. Players cannot even do this at their leisure because they are given a limited amount of time (which can be varied according to a player's ability) to solve the mystery. The only context, and the only real point of the exercise, is to find out where Carmen is as quickly as possible.

The problem with games such as *Carmen Sandiego* is that they provide no framework into which students can fit the facts they learn. Instead, people and places pop up as isolated phenomena that are discarded as soon as they have served their purposes. To discover, for example, that "If that's the Eiffel Tower, Carmen must have gone to Paris" does little to teach children about the geography of France. Children are much more likely to develop an understanding of geography if they are first taught to find their way around their own neighborhood, and then create their own maps of where they have walked and what they have seen.

While visiting an inner-city school in Boston, I noticed that during a geography lesson the teacher took several minutes to draw out of the students the name of the river (the Charles River) that flows through their city. Every student in the fourth grade would have known this fact, along with many other observations about the river, if they had simply been taken on a field trip to walk along its banks.

Our schools spend vast sums of money on the integration of technology, the effects of which are often counterproductive. Computer drills might help, in some cases, to raise students' standardized test scores, but such measures are a narrow form of assessment. Test scores, whether delivered electronically or not, do not even begin to hint at the potential in each child.

5

Computers Can Make Students More Interested in Learning

Leslie Bennetts

Leslie Bennetts was a writer for FamilyPC *magazine when she wrote this article.*

Many schools around the nation are using computers to make schoolwork exciting and challenging rather than tedious. The most successful of these schools use computers and the Internet to engage students in projects that show them how their knowledge and skills can be used in the real world. For example, students in one school created multimedia content for a CD-ROM designed to attract new businesses to their community, while another school held mock federal and statewide elections in which students voted online and used the Internet to monitor the real-life 2000 elections. Programs like these demonstrate the potential that technology has to make education more effective, engaging, and relevant.

D ropout rates are down and test scores are up. Students are engaged in learning and their self-esteem is soaring. So what's really going on within the classroom walls of the country's top wired schools?

Once upon a time, back in the olden days, kids used to exult about getting out of school, celebrating their release from drudgery by singing "No more pencils, no more books!"—or so the schoolyard ditty would have it. These days, with the explosion of technology that's revolutionizing education around the country, many students are now eager to stay after school, competing for access to all the high-tech equipment that's opening up so many new opportunities to them.

For younger kids, technology is transforming the schoolwork their older siblings sometimes regarded as tedious into challenging games and activities. For high-school students, technology may banish once and for all the tired questions about relevance. Even the most rebellious adolescents are aware of the real-world value of the skills and experience they're getting in wired schools.

Teachers who have mastered the art of integrating technology into the curriculum also deserve credit. For a closer look at some of the ways educators are transforming American schools, here are six outstanding examples from [*FamilyPC's* 2000] Top 100 Wired Schools—two elementary, two middle, and two high schools that have applied creativity as well as resources to the educational challenges of the 21st century.

High-tech schools make learning fun

Camelot Elementary School, Lewiston, Idaho. With computers offering Internet access in every classroom, Camelot Elementary School is a bustling hub of technology-related activity. Every student has a Web page—4th-, 5th-, and 6th-graders actually design their own—where they publish their stories, illustrations, and schoolwork so parents, relatives, and friends can keep track of what they're doing. Some 6th-grade students also publish an online school newspaper and yearbook using digital cameras and scanners to add photos and pictures to their articles.

The videoconferencing labs give students the opportunity to talk to children from other parts of the state, or even farther afield; two 5th-grade classes chatted with kids in Japan. "It's really fun for the kids to be able to see who they're talking to" says Debbie Kuntz, the school's computer technologist.

[At Camelot Elementary School] every student has a Web page—4th-, 5th-, and 6th-graders actually design their own.

But it's more than just fun; the technology helps students enhance their understanding of current events. This year, 6th-graders and their Idaho "pen pals" are discussing a state proposal to remove dams on the Snake River; the environmentally friendly plan to encourage salmon breeding could have an adverse impact on the livelihood of some state residents, including their parents. "The kids are learning that people in other parts of the state are impacted in different ways by the same issue," says Kuntz.

A favorite high-tech activity at Camelot is the so-called Monster Project, which builds skills in areas as diverse as art, outlining, descriptive writing, and Web-page creation and design. This year, 3rd-graders become e-mail pals with kids from another school district and play the guess-what-my-monster-looks-like game. First, the children draw vividly colored monsters. Then they use Inspiration software, which helps students develop ideas and organize thinking, to outline a description of their monsters. Based on their outlines, students write paragraphs detailing their monster's unique features, which they send to their e-mail pals.

The recipients, who have not seen the pictures of the monsters, draw what they think their pal's monster looks like. Then they send a description of their drawing to the creator. The pen pals write back and forth, asking questions or clarifying important details. (If the monster has three eyes, are they arranged in a triangle or a straight line?)

The culmination of the project is a picnic at a local park. The kids from the different schools, who have not met before, line up holding their monster pictures and try to find their monster twin. After the picnic, students create Web pages about the project, including their monster descriptions, their own drawing, and the drawing that their pal made. The pals continue their e-mail relationships for the rest of the school year.

Delano Optional School, Memphis, Tennessee. Delano is a magnet school in an inner-city neighborhood where the student population is 96 percent Black. Delano is also a Co-nect school (www.co-nect.net), in which technology and real-world projects are integrated into its curriculum.

One project that the entire school participates in every year is Delano TeleVision. Students in the 4th, 5th, and 6th grades produce a daily news show, the "Noon News" which is broadcast to every classroom via closed-circuit TV. Each week, a team of students fills 15 positions, from director and producer to sound technicians, visual designers, and weather announcers, with each successive crew training the next one. They use digital audio/video mixers to switch between the cameras and the computers for different video shots. Broadcasts run from 10 to 25 minutes and include world news. Each day a student is chosen to say the Pledge of Allegiance. Another daily feature is the "Question of the Day" an educational trivia question, such as "Who was the tallest president of the United States?" Various students are also recognized on the program for outstanding achievements.

Since Delano adopted the Co-nect approach to education four years ago, learning is based on team projects that take place throughout the school year. Each project culminates in an activity in which students are required to use various forms of technology, including computers, printers, video cameras, digital cameras, scanners, laser disc players, and the Internet. Each class presents at least one of its activities on the "Noon News." At the end of the year, the school celebrates students' achievements with a Technology Fair, where students create traditional cardboard displays and multimedia presentations that show their use of technology. Parents and friends are invited to attend the fair.

Lynn Williams, Delano's technology coordinator, says she has seen significant changes in the students' teamwork, motivation, and self-esteem as a result of the school's commitment to technology. "Technology helps students who learn best through hands-on experiences" she says. "We've had students every year for whom Delano TeleVision is their sole motivation for coming to school. Kids try to keep their grades up so they can make the team. For students who are doing poorly, just being in there boosts their self-esteem incredibly."

Community-based school projects

Fayette Middle School, Fayette, Alabama. The Fayette Middle School, located in a small rural town in northwest Alabama, has endured the loss of some important businesses in recent years, with a concomitant loss of jobs. Last spring [2000] local leaders asked the school to create a CD-ROM highlighting all the good things the town of Fayette has to offer, with the idea of using it to advertise the community and attract new businesses.

"Eighth-grade students took digital pictures of the park, the courthouse, the library, the businesses," says Melanie Trull, the school's technology coordinator. "They also interviewed city leaders, including the mayor, and wrote descriptions of the businesses and the educational and recreational facilities in town. They used HyperStudio software to create a multimedia slide show, burned it into a CD, and presented it to the city council and other local leaders, who were very impressed."

"Anytime kids break down the classroom walls and see the wider world, they become more motivated learners."

So were the students. "It had a positive effect on the kids" says Trull. "They saw that they could use technology for their careers; I don't think it had ever crossed their minds before."

Will Etheridge, one of the students who worked on the multimedia project, says the experience had a profound effect on him and his schoolmates. "We were honored that they let us do this, and it was a lot of fun getting to work with the city council and helping them to organize the project," adds Etheridge, who was 14 when he participated in it last year. "The local TV station even offered us summer jobs. It's given us an opportunity to look into a new world. We're going to be dealing with computers a lot, and I'm glad the school has given us the opportunity to learn about them at an early age. It's educational, but it's also fun."

This year [2001] one of the school's community-based projects is to create a print pamphlet, multimedia presentation, and Web site for LEAF (Local Education Advancement Foundation). The 8th-grade students in Trull's multimedia class will take digital photos of past LEAF projects and use graphic design and multimedia software to show how community leaders work closely with the town's businesses and schools to fund local educational needs.

Every classroom in Fayette Middle School has at least one computer with Internet access. The school also has four computer labs that in the spring are often filled with students using SAT-prep software. "The kids would rather practice their skills on the computer than sit in a classroom and do worksheets," says Trull. "Our SAT scores have even gone up, and I think technology has been a part of that."

Audubon Middle School, Milwaukee, Wisconsin. An urban school with a predominantly minority student body, 98 percent of whom are bussed to school from the inner city, Audubon has made enormous strides in getting wired over the last few years. Seven years ago, the school had 15 Apple computers. Today, every classroom has teacher and student workstations, and the school has four computer labs, a video lab, a computer-aided design (CAD) lab, a graphic arts lab, and two distance-learning sites. All students receive instruction in the technical and ethical aspects of sharing files on a network, desktop publishing, hypermedia, digital photography, digital video, graphic arts, and CAD, among other subjects.

"When the planning committee decided to make technology the tool for instruction about five years ago, the administration made it pretty clear to the staff: 'This is a train coming down the track; either hop on it or get run over'" says Cary Werner, Audubon's technology coordinator. "Our goal is to make good workers in the 21st century who can think critically and communicate productively, and technology is our tool for that. When the kids see that there are computers in every classroom and labs on every floor, they come in with the expectation that it's going to be cool. When they hold a camera and download the images into a presentation they've created, they own that, a lot more than they own a worksheet somebody gave them to fill out."

[In September 2000] several 6th-grade social studies classes from Audubon, under the instruction of Karen Jagmin, cooperated with a group of 10th-graders from another Milwaukee public school in a project involving the Olympics in Sydney. The students picked Olympic sports they were interested in, researched the sport and its athletes, and kept track of the United States' performance in the competitions using the Internet, newspapers, online magazines, CD-ROMs, and TV. Every day they e-mailed a group of high-school students in Sydney, who would respond to their questions.

"Technology makes learning exciting and gives students opportunities to use skills many of them already have mastered from growing up with computers."

Among the topics the students discussed via e-mail were whether other countries make icons out of sports figures the way the United States does, and how cultural differences affect the ways in which athletes are selected and trained. The Audubon students made spreadsheets and graphs showing everything from the medal counts to the shot-put distances, and they wrote summaries explaining their data. They then worked in cooperative groups to create PowerPoint presentations about their experiences to share with other students in their grade and with their 10th-grade partners via Audubon's distance-learning network.

"Our kids had a good time with it," says Werner. "They didn't know how much they didn't know, and they learned a lot about judging and point systems, which worked into their mathematics instruction. Anytime kids break down the classroom walls and see the wider world, they become more motivated learners."

Innovative Web-based projects

Granby High School, Norfolk, Virginia. Last fall, Fred Hartnett, an advanced placement government teacher at Granby, taught an entire unit using Web-based assignments. His students participated in the Youth Leadership Initiative sponsored by the University of Virginia (www.youthleadership. net). The kids registered online for a statewide mock election to vote for presidential, congressional, and senatorial candidates. One class member attended a training session at the university to serve as a student facilitator. Each student used the Internet to research a state's past presidential voting history and current polling projections. The unit culminated in an election-night sleepover at the school in which students tracked the results of the [2000] election, including the cliffhanger presidential race. "A number of kids were saying, 'I'll never miss another election,' because of the drama of just being involved," says Michael J. Caprio, the principal. "It was very valuable; they saw what the system was all about. They saw democracy work. They lived history."

This past school year [2000] was the third since Granby upgraded its facilities to provide state-of-the-art technology. The school instituted a number of Internet-related programs, such as BoxerMath.com—interactive multimedia tutorials that encourage kids to explore algebra, geometry, and trigonometry concepts themselves.

The results have been impressive. Since getting wired, Caprio reports, "Our standardized state test scores have skewed up, our SAT scores have improved, and attendance has improved. I have students who come to school to go on the Internet. If this excites the kids and turns them on, that's great. Our dropout rates have decreased and so have suspensions and expulsions. Students come to school more ready to learn and we have the technology to challenge them."

Gulf Coast High School, Naples, Florida. In order to get wired, most schools have to undergo disruptive renovations to their existing facilities. Gulf Coast, which opened three years ago, is in the enviable position of having been created and designed with state-of-the-art technology from the outset. In addition to 10 computer labs, every classroom has computer stations and a teacher presentation station so that technology can be integrated fully into the curriculum.

Gulf Coast's approach to learning was designed around new ways to utilize technology. "One of the concepts for our school was that it would not be a traditional school where kids would sit and think, 'Why am I learning this?'" says Elaine Gates, one of the school's media specialists. "When I was in school, we sat at desks and the teacher stood at the front and talked; students took notes and tests. But most kids learn by doing, not just by listening. Technology makes learning exciting and gives students opportunities to use skills many of them already have mastered from growing up with computers."

In Gulf Coast's interdisciplinary approach to learning, teachers from more than one academic area work together to design a teaching unit. One recent project was called Legends, an unusual collaboration between the English and physical education departments in which students studied the tale of King Arthur. "Students in the English classes took different themes: King Arthur in stained glass, King Arthur in literature, King Arthur in Broadway plays, and so on," Gates says. "They researched their topics using the Internet and created presentations that included 3D animation, sound, and video. The physical education classes researched medieval and Renaissance dance and sporting events like jousting. They learned medieval dances, which they taught to the students in the English class. The results were filmed and are being made into a CD-ROM."

In fact, the phys ed department infuses technology into all of its fitness activities. "Every single one of our PE courses uses video and digital photography in many ways, including analyzing movement in sports and presenting information on fitness and health," says Gates. "Students research a topic such as jet skiing, kayaking, or surfing, and make a Power-Point presentation about that fitness activity. They also take digital pictures of the correct way to use each weight and exercise machine in the school's fitness room and they post the images on the school's Web site."

The phys ed department uses TriFit, a computer-based analysis system in which exercise bikes, heart-rate monitors, strength machines, and other equipment are all connected to a PC. While hooked up to the equipment, an individual undergoes a series of tests to measure strength, flexibility, and aerobic capacity. The computer prints an analysis of the person's fitness and life risks and can customize an exercise program, diet, and nutritional information for that individual.

"Technology is an innovative way for kids to learn the things they need to know academically and also to learn the tools of technology," says Gates. "The kids almost demand it."

6

Computer-Assisted Education Can Undermine Serious Study

Joanne K. Olson and Michael P. Clough

Joanne K. Olson and Michael P. Clough are assistant professors at the Center for Excellence in Science and Mathematics Education at Iowa State University.

Computer-assisted education is merely the latest in a series of attempts to use technology to improve education. However, while computers may make classrooms more "fun," in many ways technology hinders students' ability to truly learn. For example, calculators and word processing spell-checkers do not help students learn arithmetic or spelling. Student-oriented technologies are often "black boxes"—they do not require students to understand the concepts or processes that underlie these technologies. Computers and other technologies make complex tasks easier, but when used in the classroom, they ultimately reduce students' motivation to learn complex concepts.

In our increasingly polarized culture, taking a middle position on important issues is becoming more difficult. Few seem to appreciate when individuals position themselves on a fence dividing two opposing camps, and interestingly, those on either side of the fence often demand allegiance to one position or the other. "You can't sit on the fence," such moderates are told, despite their often being able to see farther from that vantage point than those standing on either side of the fence. So with some concern of being labeled "Luddites" by those who champion technology in the classroom and "technophiles" by those opposing its intrusion, we take the position that although technology could assist teachers and students in making schooling effective, in many ways it exacerbates current problems.

Deep and robust learning requires serious study

Developing deep, robust, and long-term understanding of science concepts is but one of the aims of the National Science Education Standards. Optimally, students should also gain an understanding of the nature of science and the attributes and skills that make for effective science inquiry. The task is daunting, and reaching those goals will be impossible without a deep understanding of what learning means and of the teacher's essential role in that process. Understanding how students learn—and why they sometimes don't—is the foundation of informed teaching.

Constructivist learning theory emphasizes that students use their pre-existing knowledge to grapple with and make sense of experience, and thus teaching should center on what learners know and how they make meaning. In the past decade, constructivism has received almost exclusive attention in education literature, and a number of radical constructivist views have emerged that are now, for good reasons, being attacked. Constructivism has come to mean so many different things to different people that it no longer conveys a specific meaning. But the foundations of constructivist learning theory are well supported and, if used wisely, help make sense out of the complexities associated with learning and teaching.

First, learning is an active process, and for learning to occur students must be mentally active—selectively taking in and attending to information, and connecting and comparing it to prior knowledge and additional incoming information in an attempt to make sense of what is being received. Second, because the incoming sensory input is primarily organized by the individual receiving it, the intended meaning is often not communicated intact. Third, knowledge that a student brings to current instruction may help or hinder the creation of meaning similar to what was intended by that external source. Fourth, students' prior knowledge that is at odds with the intended learning (meaning) is, at times, extremely resistant to change. That is, in attempting to make sense of instruction, students interpret and sometimes modify incoming stimuli so that they fit with or connect to what they already believe. Fifth, as the number of links made to new learning increases, the likelihood of long-term and meaningful learning increases. These postulates help explain how learning occurs, and they also raise concerns regarding whether particular technologies promote or inhibit intended learning.

Computers . . . and other forms of technology do not promote and often hinder deep conceptual understanding.

Clearly, effective science teaching is highly interactive. Such teaching makes explicit students' relevant prior knowledge, engenders active mental struggling with that prior knowledge and new experiences, and encourages metacognition. Without this, students rarely create meaning similar to that of the scientific community. And that is also why most textbooks, audiovisual and multimedia materials, laser discs, computers, and other forms of technology do not promote and often hinder deep conceptual understanding. They do a poor job of making apparent and playing off students' prior ideas, engendering deep reflection, and promoting understanding of complex content. Worse yet, technology often undermines such serious study.

Technology's tendency to undermine serious study

Neil Postman writes in *The End of Education* that all technological change is a Faustian bargain—that every advantage is tied to a corresponding disadvantage. To illustrate this point, we have chosen two unintended and rarely considered consequences of technology that appear to us to undermine the serious thinking and metacognition necessary for deep, robust learning.

Education and entertainment

All sorts of technologies fascinate students and have the potential to grab and maintain their attention in ways that interacting with a teacher, reading a book, seriously discussing ideas with other students, and thinking about their own thinking cannot. One has only to look at the hours children spend spellbound in front of a television or surfing the Web (which by no coincidence is looking more and more like television) to see how rapidly changing sensory information plays to our biological bias attuning us to changes in our immediate environment. Technology not only entertains, it also speeds up life by reducing the time we spend on dull, tedious tasks. Calculators, graphing software, spelling and grammar checkers, educational software, and a host of other devices are invaluable tools to save us from mundane tasks. Not surprisingly, students, parents, and even educators have enthusiastically and often uncritically endorsed technology in education. However, the wholly unforeseen consequence is the now pervasive attitude that learning should largely be fun and entertaining, or at least not a struggle. Over fifteen years ago, Postman warned that whether particular technologies teach students their ABCs and how to count is of minor importance compared with what they teach students about learning and schooling. Using *Sesame Street* as merely one example, he writes:

> We now know that "Sesame Street" encourages children to love school only if school is like "Sesame Street." Which is to say, we now know that "Sesame Street" undermines what the traditional idea of schooling represents. Whereas a classroom is a place of social interaction, the space in front of a television is a private preserve. Whereas in a classroom, one may ask a teacher questions, one can ask nothing of a television screen. Whereas school is centered on the development of language, television demands attention to images. Whereas attending school is a legal requirement, watching television is an act of choice. Whereas in school, one fails to attend to the teacher at the risk of punishment, no penalties exist for failing to attend to the television screen. Whereas to behave oneself in school means to observe rules

of public decorum, television watching requires no such observances, has no concept of public decorum. Whereas in a classroom, fun is never more than a means to an end, on television it is the end in itself.

The underlying attitude that education should be enjoyable and entertaining, or at the very least not deliberate and measured, makes much of what we know about effective teaching appear stale and old-fashioned. Yet engaging prior knowledge, grappling with new experiences, struggling to make sense of those new experiences, thinking about thinking, making new connections, and finding that prior connections no longer make sense are serious and difficult struggles requiring much effort, diligence, and perseverance on the student's part. Those activities are precisely what television, radio, computers, calculators, graphing software, and many other forms of technology often circumvent. Thus one of the most pervasive outcomes of technology use is that students acquire the belief that learning should not be a struggle and that good teaching will make learning enjoyable and easy.

One of the most pervasive outcomes of technology use is that students acquire the belief that learning should not be a struggle.

The practical outcome of this change in student attitudes is that teachers at all levels are increasingly incorporating technologies into their classrooms to catch students' attention, but are doing so at the expense of serious study. Postman, addressing the efforts to make classrooms more entertaining, writes,

> And in the end, what will the students have learned? They will, to be sure, have learned something about [the content in question], most of which they could have learned just as well by other means. Mainly, they will have learned that learning is a form of entertainment or, more precisely, that anything worth learning can take the form of an entertainment, and ought to.

Of course, effective teaching is mentally stimulating and often enjoyable. However, meaningful learning is just as often a discomforting struggle that is rewarding only after much cognitive and emotional effort. So although technology often fascinates students, it has an unintended effect of battering habits congruent with serious learning.

Another black box

The following question was posted to high school students: "Assume you drive your vehicle 10,000 miles/yr. Gasoline averages $1.29/gallon, and your average fuel economy is 23 mpg. If you owned a vehicle with an average fuel economy of 40 mpg, how much money would you save each year in fuel costs?"

Answer from typically a quarter of students: "$219,300."
Teacher: "How much sense does that make?"
Student: "That's the number my calculator gave me."
Teacher: "Do you believe everything your calculator tells you?"
Student: (Look of bewilderment)
Teacher: "If I could save $219,300 each year by buying a more fuel-efficient vehicle, I'd use public transportation and retire a millionaire in five years."

Paulos laments that the way mathematics is taught in schools contributes to what he terms "innumeracy"—the lack of a basic sense of numbers and what they mean. Technology often impedes scientific literacy in the same way that it contributes to innumeracy. Despite recommendations to make technology "transparent," technology is often a "black box" that either misleads students into thinking they need not understand conceptually what the technology is doing for them or, worse, promotes serious misunderstanding of the concept under investigation.

For instance, researchers found that even the brightest students in a high school physics classroom did not understand the basic concept of an electrical circuit despite two months of instruction on electricity. When asked how to make a bulb light, one student thought that a bulb holder was a necessary part of a circuit. When trying to light the bulb, the student asked the interviewer, "Can I use the little piece we used in class?" When asked why she needed the bulb holder, she stated, "It carries the charge or something. . . . I don't think it will light without it." The presence of this rudimentary piece of technology and the black box nature of it not only clouded the purpose of the bulb holder, it created a misconception regarding the basic concept of a circuit, on which many other concepts are built.

Students' use of technology often hides their misunderstanding and interferes with learning and teaching.

Equipment is often used before students have seriously grappled with the concepts under study. As a result, they can perceive the technology to be a necessary part of the concept, or worse, have little understanding about what they are doing. The first author recently interacted with a group of middle school students working on a water quality project. Equipped with expensive calculator-based laboratory equipment, the students were excitedly putting probes into the water and recording results. The students were motivated to do the activity, and the teacher was receiving district acclaim for being at the "cutting edge" of science education. When asked what they were doing, a group of students answered, "We're putting this probe in the water, reading the number, and writing it down in the box." "What does the number tell you?" The student looked at her paper and read her answer: "Dissolved oxygen concentration." "What's that?" "I don't know," the student responded, "I just write down the number." The second author observed a tenth-grade class performing gel electrophoresis and had the following dialogue with a group of students:

Observer: "So what are you doing in this lab activity?"
Student: "Gel electrophoresis."
Observer: "What's that?"
Student: (pointing at apparatus) "Watching the blue dot move through the gel."
Observer: "What's the blue dot?"
Student: "I don't know."
Observer: "Why is it moving?"
Student: "Electricity. Current."
Observer: "How does the current cause the blue dot to move?"
Student: "We don't know." (Nervous laughter)

M. Almy warned teachers that having students engage in manipulative or verbal operations that they cannot engage in mentally tends to erect knowledge superstructures that crumble under the slightest cognitive stress. Incorporating technology before students mentally grasp the underlying fundamental concepts does just that. Of course, technology can at times motivate students to learn the underlying concepts, but in the examples provided above, the technology was so far beyond students' conceptual understanding that it could not motivate them in that way.

Technology's inherent labor-saving bias encourages students and teachers to skip conceptual understanding. Many champions of technology in the classroom speak glowingly of projects that involve students in using multiple media to complete tasks formerly done by hand. R. Pearlman enthusiastically describes such a project:

> Last year kids at 200 schools throughout the country, working in teams, took water samples from local rivers, lakes, ponds, open fields, and water taps. Back in their classrooms the teams measured the pH levels of the water, recorded the results, and took averages for the samples. Then each team entered their results into a specially designed software program that allowed the class to average their results and then telecommunicate them, via modem, to a national computer.
>
> The next day the results of all sites were available for download from the national computer to the classroom computer, where they could be printed out and where special mapping software could generate color-coded maps of acid rain levels. Students then discussed the findings and communicated their analysis, again via modem to an expert at the National Oceanic and Atmospheric Administration, who wrote back and compared their findings to current scientific analyses.

What is tragically missing from the account is any description of what the teacher's role was, how students were engaged in making meaning from this experience, whether they understood what they were reporting, or why they were even doing the activity. In our excitement for using technology we have to remind ourselves that students' use of technology often hides their misunderstanding and interferes with learning and teaching.

Teachers are the key

These examples underscore the importance of the teacher. In the presence of technology, however, the teacher's role in promoting learning becomes more difficult, as the black box nature of the technology often works to conceal students' thinking about the fundamental concepts. Overemphasizing technology, like overemphasizing curricula, neglects the teacher in favor of changing the activities that students do. Despite the critical role of curricula, the evidence is clear that teachers are the most influential factor in educational change. The bottom line is that teachers, not technology, make exemplary science programs. J.A. Langer and A.N. Applebee, after observing how teachers assimilated new writing activities into their old ways of thinking, wrote,

> For those who wish to reform education through the introduction of new curricula, the results suggest a different message. We are unlikely to make fundamental changes in instruction simply by changing curricula and activities without attention to the purposes the activities serve for the teacher as well as for the student. It may be much more important to give teachers new frameworks for understanding what to count as learning than it is to give them new activities or curricula. . . .[T]o summarize bluntly, given traditional notions of instruction, it may be impossible to implement successfully the approaches we have championed.

Teachers translate curriculum into a form ready for classroom application and decide what, how, and why to learn. As E.W. Eisner writes, "In the final analysis, what teachers do in the classroom and what students experience define the educational process." The principles of effective teaching are not changed by the presence or absence of technology. In light of how individuals learn, teaching for conceptual understanding is an extremely interactive undertaking, requiring teachers to know their students' ideas and to engage students in meaning-making based on those ideas. That requires effectively questioning, using wait time, offering supportive nonverbal cues, actively listening, responding to students in ways that promote further thinking, and structuring activities to keep students mentally engaged.

Issues when considering technology in the classroom

Be wary of introducing technology too far removed from students' conceptual understanding. Teachers should carefully consider whether students' prior knowledge is sufficient to understand what the technology is doing for them and whether the novel concepts introduced by the technology can be linked to their prior understanding. If the distance between students' prior knowledge and the technology is too great for mental engagement to occur, then the technology becomes a black box. Students may be perplexed as to why they need to understand the concepts, inasmuch as the technology does the work for them. In this case, the technology actually reduces motivation to learn complex content.

Technology should not determine the content or activity. The availability of technology does not justify its inclusion in the classroom. Unfortunately, as technology becomes more widely available at lower cost, teachers are increasingly including activities in their curricula that are neither developmentally appropriate nor coherent with other topics. Introductory high school biology and even middle school life science students are now performing gel electrophoresis and polymerase chain reactions simply because the technology has recently become available at reasonable expense. Never mind that most students have little or no prior chemistry experience and have significant difficulty conceptually understanding the molecular structure and function of DNA and proteins. Requiring students to use such technology may seem interesting and "cutting edge," but how well students can really understand what they are doing is questionable, given their difficulties with the fundamental concepts that such technology is based on. Simply because technology permits particular activities to be done doesn't mean that they should be done.

Teachers are wise to consider both the gains and the losses when introducing technology in the classroom.

Consider how the technology will promote desired student goals. Although comprehending the fundamental ideas in science is important, other student goals are just as critical to teachers and their students' understanding of science. All goals need not be facilitated in every classroom activity, but teachers do need to consider how the introduction of a particular technology will help or hinder each goal. As we have argued, technologies may promote student interest but retard conceptual understanding. Some technologies promote particular ways of communication while trivializing others. All technologies have biases, and the teacher must discern those biases when deciding what to incorporate and how and when to use it.

Consider your rationale for using technology. If entertainment is the primary purpose, consider other options. If the primary advantage of using the technology is that it will be fun for students or more "motivating," seriously consider why this is so. We think you will find that technology often diminishes the need to attend seriously to prior knowledge, to use metacognitive strategies, question prior ideas, generate examples, compare alternative solutions, grapple with new experiences, make sense of those new experiences, make new connections, and analyze whether prior connections continue to make sense. If the primary advantage of the technology is student interest, what are students being motivated to deliberately study, and how effectively does the technology motivate them to do this? However, if the technology can do most of those things while being enjoyable, then incorporating it is appropriate.

Consider what is gained and what is lost by using the technology. Because all technology is a Faustian bargain, teachers are wise to consider both the gains and the losses when introducing technology in the classroom. Students who engage in e-mail activities with a distant class may gain keyboarding skills and print-based communication skills, but they may lose verbal skills such as speaking and listening, as well as handwriting skills. Teachers who understand the gains as well as the losses can better make informed decisions about whether, when, and how technology should be used. The teacher may value the skills gained through the email project, for example, but will need to engage students in additional activities that rely on handwriting and speaking and listening skills.

How does the technology promote or inhibit understanding students' thinking? Because of the black box nature of most technology, student thinking is often hidden. When students use a calculator or computer to solve problems, their procedures are often not available for teacher diagnosis. Teachers can falsely assume that students understand the concept because they have correctly solved a problem. Effective teachers work to understand students' thinking behind their answers and how technology helps or hinders it.

Any technology should be a means to a more noble end, not an end in itself. D.G. Hawkridge, J. Jaworske, and H. McMahon identify four main reasons that are cited for using technology in schools. The first reason is social: students need to know how to use technology because technology is everywhere. A second reason is vocational: students need to learn technology because they may need it in their future careers. The third reason is pedagogic: students can learn better from a computer. Fourth, some reformers assert that computers themselves can be a catalyst for systemic change in education. None of these assertions, however, is adequately supported by research. The most attractive rationale for including technology in the classroom is pedagogic—that students can learn better from using computers. Yet D.P. Ely found that research on student learning with technology is inadequate, contradictory, and inconclusive.

These questionable rationales for including technology in the classroom, however, have been so widely and uncritically accepted that little serious discussion about them occurs. Technology is often included in schools as an end in itself. Technology is perceived as good, and those who do not embrace it are given labels such as "resisters" and "Luddites." L. Cuban argues against those who use the above rationales and asserts that doubts about the inclusion of computers in the classroom have received inadequate attention. As Postman argues, the inclusion of computers has received inadequate attention because

> educators confuse the teaching of how to use technology with technology education. . . . Technology education does not imply a negative attitude toward technology. It does imply a critical attitude. Technology education aims at students' learning about what technology helps us to do and what it hinders us from doing; it is about how technology uses us, for good or ill, and about how it has used people in the past, for good or ill. It is about how technology creates new worlds, for good or ill.

Worse yet, the rhetoric of technology education as it often appears in the literature moves the dialogue away from such issues.

Examining the nature of technology

In science education, understanding the nature of science is a primary component of all reform documents. Science education is not simply about learning science content; its more important mission is to help students understand what science is, its limitations, how it affects and is affected by society, and how scientists and the scientific community work to generate knowledge. Likewise, meaningful technology education is far more than learning how to use technology to further other ends. It includes a rich understanding of what technology is, how and why technology is developed, how scientists and technologists operate as a social group, and how society itself directs, reacts to, and is unwittingly changed by new technologies. Education must move beyond its narrow focus of simply teaching students the mechanics of technology and blindly ignoring its more meaningful consequences. The concept of technology education must be broadened to include the nature of technology and to confront questions like those raised by Postman:

- For every advantage of technology, what is the corresponding disadvantage?
- How are the advantages and disadvantages of particular new technologies distributed unevenly?
- What is the underlying philosophy of particular technologies? For example, how do particular technologies change the way we think and act?
- How does new technology compete with older technology in regard to how we think of the world?
- What are the intellectual and emotional biases of particular technologies?
- What are the sensory, social, and content biases of particular technologies?
- What goals are promoted? What goals are ignored?
- How are other technologies impacted?
- How does this technology change the way we view schooling?
- How does the technology promote or inhibit thinking?

The cautionary perspective we take raises questions about the "cognitive biases and social effects" of technologies on education and how they often undermine what we know about effective teaching and learning. Our view from atop the fence has shown us that although technology has great potential to motivate and engage students, it can also change their fundamental ideas about the purposes of schools, potentially to their own detriment. Further, because of its black box nature, technology in classrooms often circumvents critical requirements of learning and can hide or even inhibit students' thinking. The teacher's role is critical, and attention must focus on how teachers engage students in making sense of their experiences. In addition, we need to address critical questions regarding the nature of technology and the inclusion of technology in classrooms and to carefully consider the Faustian bargain we make.

7

Computer-Assisted Education Benefits Young Children

The Children's Partnership

The Children's Partnership is a national nonprofit organization whose mission is to inform leaders and the public about the needs of America's 70 million children, and to engage them in ways that benefit children.

The information age has arrived, and good parents should prepare their children for it by promoting computer literacy as soon as children are ready for it. Children as young as two and three can play with a computer in the home, and by age eight children can begin using the Internet for school reports. Parents should especially encourage girls to become comfortable with computers—by the teen years many girls lose interest in information technology—since computer literacy is important for both men and women.

The information age is arriving at lightning speed. Children and young people are among the most active citizens of the new era, and are often first in their family to use the new media. Some parents and other guardians of young people are enthusiastic about the new technologies; others desperately hope these changes will just go away.

However, there is little doubt that computers are here to stay and that they're changing the way young people learn, play, and get ready for their work life.

- By the year 2000, an estimated 60 percent of new jobs in America will require technological skills and computer know-how.
- In the early 1990s, workers with computer skills earned 10–15% more than workers without such skills.

And children are increasingly using new technologies in their schools, libraries, homes, and communities.

- Estimates show that in May 1997, nearly 10 million children were

The Children's Partnership, "The Parent's Guide to the Information Superhighway," www.childrenspartnership.org, May 1998. Copyright © 1998 by The Children's Partnership. Reproduced by permission.

online either at home, at school, or in the community—a five-fold increase from fall 1995.
- For the 50 million children now in U.S. elementary and secondary schools, 27% of classrooms have Internet access and 78% of schools have some kind of access to the Internet.

In addition, parents understand that computer skills are important. In fact, 89% of parents believe computer skills are important to educational success.

But parents face uncharted territory, and the technologies are evolving so quickly it seems hard to get a handle on what this new territory really is. One parent commented:

> It's like being illiterate in a world of readers. We don't know enough about what's out there to know what to be concerned about.

In addition, not all parents can afford a computer in the home, and not all schools are yet integrating technology into learning—creating a gap between children who are prepared for information-era jobs and those who aren't.

How can a parent teach, when there's so much to learn? This new challenge may seem unlike any other you've faced before as a parent. But, in fact, many of the answers lie in common sense, some basic experience, regular vigilance, and sensible guidelines for children.

What computers and the information superhighway can and cannot do

They can help children learn skills using information resources and technology such as problem-solving, fact-gathering, analysis, and writing on computers—skills that employers will seek from future workers (today's young people). They can also help young people learn computer programming and other marketable skills.

They can open up new worlds of rich learning experiences to children through schools, libraries, and home. For example, children can work on a school project with other children in countries thousands of miles away—or gather information from and try out their ideas with renowned scientists, authors, or business leaders. And "electronic pen pals"—either relatives or new online friends—from opposite ends of the planet can e-mail each other almost instantly. They can increase access to children who have been shut out. Children in poor or rural school districts can use online services to visit museums, cities, and wildlife preserves they would not otherwise get to see. Children with disabilities can participate more fully in learning, in art programs, and in socializing.

They can increase access to children who have been shut out. Children in poor or rural school districts can use online services to visit museums, cities, and wildlife preserves they would not otherwise get to see. Children with disabilities can participate more fully in learning, in art programs, and in socializing.

Computer and online time alone can't make your child an honor student. Children learn best when they receive individualized attention and encouragement from teachers and parents. Every kind of technology—from the blackboard to slide presentations to cable TV in the classroom to CD-ROMs—is simply a tool whose effectiveness depends on using it well.

Computers alone won't make your child a well-rounded, successful adult. Children still need the balance that comes from outdoor activities, friends and family, solid academic skills, and healthy relationships with strong adult role models.

Computers and the information superhighway can be a way for you to spend more time with your child on educational and recreational activities. Research shows that family involvement in a child's education is one of the most important ingredients for success. Spending time online with your child can be a way to connect with what he or she is learning in school and to stay involved. Computers can also help you expose your child to information and experiences that you value.

Information literacy skills will increasingly be expected of young people.

Online technologies can also be a way for you to stay in touch with your child's teachers, school schedules, and homework assignments. Increasingly, schools are offering parents access to important school information via e-mail and online school discussion groups. This can be especially helpful for parents whose work schedules make it hard for them to meet with teachers or be at school during the school day.

So, why should you care about computers and the information superhighway? First, because information literacy skills will increasingly be expected of young people. Young people fluent in information resources will likely have advantages in the workplace. Second, this new resource may hold special educational and other opportunities for your child—as the online world can bring diverse experiences to young people. And, finally, more and more children are taking the lead to get online—and need strong parental guidance to use this new medium as a rich opportunity for learning. . . .

When are children ready for computer-assisted education?

Very little formal research has been done to understand how information technology affects children of different ages and when is the "right time" to start various activities. Also, children differ in their development and maturity—so parents should first consider their own child's emotional development and abilities. But common sense, combined with advice from child development experts, suggests some age-appropriate guidelines.

Unlike some other areas of a child's growth, a parent should not treat computer use as a developmental milestone. There are no "shoulds" in this arena like "a child should walk by 15 months." The main thing to keep in mind is that the online world offers children a new set of experiences, another world to explore. It is also a new resource to help satisfy a child's seemingly endless curiosity and find answers to those amazing questions kids constantly come up with.

Many of the tips in this section apply to more than one age group. We have placed the tip in the age group where it is first applicable.

Ages 2–3: Computers need not play much of a role in the youngest child's life. However, it doesn't hurt for very young children to see family members using computers and enjoying themselves online—at a library, at a community center, or at home.

Stand-alone computers using CD-ROMs or other software (rather than online activities) are most likely to have what children this age need. Parenting magazines and some nonprofit organizations publish reviews of software that may be helpful.

Handy Tips
- Put your child in your lap as you "play" on the computer.
- Put your hand on your child's to show him or her the way the mouse works.
- Children like to play with the equipment: start slowly letting them learn about the keyboard (some are especially designed for children), the mouse, etc.
- Look for books and children's video programs like Sesame Street that include images of children and family members using a computer. These can provide important exposure and encourage interest.

Ages 4–7: While serious computer use isn't a priority for these youngsters, children at this age can begin to make greater use of computer games and educational products. Once again, parents of children this age can look to CD-ROMs and other computer software for early computer learning. Older children in this age group can also begin exploring online children's sections with their parents. This kind of exposure with a young child is a great way for a parent to get involved with new media. Yes, children do learn intuitively and quickly, but at this age they still depend on parents for reading and interpreting directions. This makes a shared computer experience a valuable give and take experience.

[Age 8 to 11] is when children can begin to directly experience and appreciate more fully the potential of online experiences.

Handy Tips
- Spend as much time as you can with your child while he or she uses the computer.
- Use actual experiences to demonstrate proper behavior and rules.
- Show lots of tangible results and achievements. For example, print work your child has done on the computer.
- Share an e-mail address with your child, so you can oversee his or her mail and discuss correspondence.
- As children go to school, check in with teachers so you can coordinate and reinforce school learning with home learning.
- Look to librarians and various parenting magazines for suggestions of good online activities.

Ages 8–11: This age is when children can begin to directly experience and appreciate more fully the potential of online experiences. Children can begin to use online encyclopedias and download pictures and graphics for school reports. They can also begin to have pen pals from many places, exchanging stories with far-away relatives and online friends, and even doing shared school projects.

It is also a very important age to set guidelines, teach values, and monitor closely what children are doing. As children move toward independence, it is important that you stay "hands-on" and help guide them to enriching and appropriate materials.

Mothers and fathers should do as much as possible to encourage girls' interest in and experience with computers.

Another important reality is that children of this age are being targeted by programmers and advertisers as an important commercial market. Media literacy—helping children evaluate content and understand what's behind advertising—is an important skill to teach.

Handy Tips
• Set very clear rules for online use and clear consequences if they are broken.
• Instruct children not to order products or give out information about themselves or their family without your permission.
• Coordinate home with school activities.
• Teach children to let you know if they encounter anything scary or unusual online.
• Help children understand the nature of commercial information and how to think about it.
• Discuss some of the unique aspects of behavior in cyberspace—like anonymity and what it means for your child and for others.
• Watch the time. Use an alarm clock or timer if you or your child lose track of time.
• Watch your phone and credit card bills.

Older children

Ages 12–14: At this age, young people can use the more sophisticated research resources of the information superhighway, accessing everything from the Library of Congress' collection to magazines and newspapers to original letters and archives from around the globe. Similarly, they can work with people in remote places on shared projects and can learn from speaking online to leading authorities on nearly any subject. In addition, many young teenagers are interested in "chatting." Most online commercial services have chat rooms that are appropriate for preteens and teenagers. There, kids can chat (via typing on their computer) to others who share their interests. A parent's job is to stay in as close touch as possible (a tough task at times).

Handy Tips
• Since children this age are more likely to explore on their own, set up clear parental rules, limits, and periodic check-ins.

- Continue to explore together as much as possible.
- Give children a basic understanding of the laws governing online behavior and the consequences of breaking them.
- Set clear rules about which chat rooms are acceptable for your teenager, and how much time can be spent there.
- Be sure your children understand the actions that can be taken if people harass them online or do anything inappropriate.
- Set a budget for online expenses and monitor it.
- Pay particular attention to games that your teenager might download or copy. Many are great fun, but others are extremely violent. Parents need to set limits about what is acceptable and what is not.

Ages 15–18: The online world is a rich resource for older teens. They can receive information about job opportunities, internships, and colleges and universities; put together multimedia reports; get specialized help with a foreign language or a subject at school; and find out just about anything else that interests them. They are also ingenious explorers, discovering new areas online and often meeting new friends. Of course, along with teens' increased curiosity, capability, and freedom come more ways to run into unpleasant or undesirable experiences. As with other activities at this age, parents can still find creative ways to keep in touch with their teenage children about online activities, and this connection is still important.

Handy Tips

- Ask your teenager for help researching topics of interest to the family (follow-up on a family discussion, family vacation, a new purchase).
- Talk to your teenager about new things online and encourage discussion of new experiences.
- Make sure your teenager knows the legal implications of online behavior.
- Watch time limits to make sure your teenager is still pursuing a well-rounded set of activities.
- If your teenager is especially interested in computers, encourage him or her to help younger children with their online explorations (try the local Boys or Girls Club) or to help a school or nonprofit organization get set up.

Girls: a league of their own

As they get older, girls use computers and online opportunities differently than boys. Many girls lose interest because the computer world, like science and math, is more oriented to males. For example, video games and other software for home computer use are overwhelmingly developed for and marketed to boys. According to a variety of reports:

- In elementary school, there is little difference between boys' and girls' computer use and ability.
- By the mid-teen years, when computer courses are typically elective, the gender gap grows and continues to widen through college and graduate school. Two and a half times as many men as women now earn computer science degrees.
- Girls use home computers for school work more than boys, and use computer games far less.

• Though in 1997, there were only two women online for every three men using the Internet, the gap is closing.

With so many jobs and much of the culture tapping into computers and information technology, mothers and fathers should do as much as possible to encourage girls' interest in and experience with computers. They should be aware that their girls will need these skills as much as boys, and should let schools and computer and content providers know they want material that appeals to girls as well as to boys.

8

Computer-Assisted Education Does Not Benefit Young Children

Alliance for Childhood

The Alliance for Childhood is a partnership of individuals and organizations committed to fostering and respecting each child's inherent right to a healthy, developmentally appropriate childhood. The following viewpoint is excerpted from the Alliance's report Fool's Gold: A Critical Look at Computers and Childhood.

Young children benefit more from interaction with the real world than with machines. Pushing young children to become computer experts has a negative effect on their creative development, which is a central part of childhood. The best way of improving early childhood education involves hiring more teachers, not buying more computers, so that all children receive adequate individual attention from teachers. Schools should implement an immediate moratorium on computers in early childhood education until the effects of such technology are more fully understood.

W hy, are we, as a nation, so enamored of computers in childhood? This one-size-fits-all fix for elementary schools does seem to meet a lot of adult needs. It makes politicians and school administrators appear decisive and progressive. It tempts overworked parents and teachers with a convenient, mesmerizing electronic babysitter. And it is irresistible to high-tech companies that hope to boost sales in the educational market.

But a machine-centered approach does not meet the developmental needs of grade-school children. Nor will it prepare them to muster the human imagination, courage, and will power they will as adults need to tackle the huge social and environmental problems looming before us.

Young children are not emotionally, socially, morally, or intellectually prepared to be pinned down to the constraining logical abstractions that computers require. This sedentary approach to learning is also unhealthy for their developing senses and growing bodies.

What's good for business is not necessarily good for children. We cannot afford educational policies that will expand the market for Microsoft, Compaq, IBM, Apple, and other companies at children's expense.

Nor can we afford the delusion that pushing young children to operate the very latest technological gadgets will somehow inoculate them from economic and cultural uncertainties in the future. Nothing can do that—certainly not soon-to-be obsolete skills in operating machines.

The importance of childhood

In the long term, what will serve them far better is a firm commitment from parents, educators, policymakers, and communities to the remarkably low-tech imperatives of childhood. Those include good nutrition, safe housing, and high-quality health care for every child—especially the one in five now growing up in poverty. They also include consistent love and nurturing for every child; active, imaginative play; a close relationship to the rest of the living world; the arts; handcrafts and hands-on lessons of every kind; and lastly time—plenty of time for children to be children.

A new respect for childhood itself, in other words, is the gift that will best prepare our children for the future's unknowns. Empowered by this gift, our children can grow into strong, resilient, creative human beings, facing tomorrow's uncertainties with competence and courage.

Some may fear that our prowess in science and technology will suffer if children are allowed to be children. The opposite is true. Consider the recent Microsoft ad, "Chasing the Future." As companies rapidly turn out one high-tech product after another, it stresses, companies and nations must "constantly replenish their long-term reserves of intellectual capital." Research, Microsoft declares, is the engine driving technical advances. So research, it adds, "has never been more important."

> *Childhood has never been more important—or more endangered by the current push to transform children into technicians.*

To the extent that's true, then so, too, has childhood never been more important—or more endangered by the current push to transform children into technicians. For childhood is the one period in the human lifespan naturally designed for pursuing the most basic science of all. That's why pushing children instead to produce PowerPoint presentations that mimic the work of adults is shortsighted. It's as shortsighted as Microsoft argues it would be for the United States to pull the plug on basic research and finance only short-term product development.

By supporting basic research, we give our most creative scientists the time they need to play with the fundamental qualities and questions of nature. In periods of great productivity, scientists say, this open-ended creative process can totally dominate their lives—whether they are working, eating, sleeping, or socializing. In short, they live their science. Granted that freedom, they generate the insights that lead to fruitful discoveries, sometimes even paradigm-shifting breakthroughs at the very edges of knowledge.

Childhood, rightly protected, is the same kind of creative process—the same kind of basic science. Children, too, need time to play with the most fundamental qualities and questions of nature—to "live" them with their whole beings: body, heart, mind, and soul. How closely related this wonder-full quest of childhood is to the expansive spirit of basic science is neatly captured in *The Scientist in the Crib: Minds, Brains, and How Children Learn*: "Our otherwise mysterious adult ability to do science may be a kind of holdover from our infant learning abilities," suggest the authors. "Adult scientists take advantage of the natural human capacities that let children learn so much so quickly. It's not that children are little scientists but that scientists are big children."

Imagination and the spirit of play are crucial to both child and adult forms of "basic science." As the anthropologist Ashley Montague noted, the most creative scientists excel in playing "let's pretend":

> The scientist says to himself, "Let me treat this 'as if' it worked that way, and we'll see what happens." He may do this entirely in his head or try it mathematically on paper or physically in the laboratory. What he is doing is using his imagination in much the same way the child does. The truth is that the highest praise one can bestow on a scientist is not to say of him that he is a fact-grubber but that he is a man of imagination. And what is imagination really? It is play— playing with ideas.

The high-tech agenda pushes children to hurry up and become skilled little technicians, experts in "accessing" other people's answers to narrow, technical questions and manipulating machine-generated images. It interrupts the creative process, the basic science, of childhood itself—the playful generation of images from one's own imagination. We do not know what the consequences of such a machine-driven education in adulthood will be. But we suspect that they will include a narrower and more shallow range of intellectual insights, a stunting of both social and technical imagination, and a drag on the productivity that stems from imaginative leaps. In short, a high-tech agenda for children seems likely to erode our most precious long-term intellectual reserves—our children's minds.

Improve schools with people, not technology

School reform is a social challenge, not a technological problem. The Education Department's own 1999 study, "Hope in Urban Education," offers powerful proof. It tells the story of nine troubled schools in high-poverty areas, all places resigned to low expectations, low achievement, and high conflict—where even the adults bickered and blamed each other. But all transformed themselves into high-achieving, cohesive communities. In the process, everyone involved—principals, teachers, other staff members, parents, and students—developed high expectations of themselves, and of each other.

The strategies that worked in these schools, the study emphasizes, were persistence, creativity in devising new ways of collaborating, maximizing the attention focused on each child, and a shared commitment to meeting the full range of children's needs.

That intensely human approach—not large expenditures on technology—is what seems to have moved all nine communities from despair to hope. Educational technology plays only a relatively minor role in the report. The words "computer" and "technology" do not even appear in the executive summary.

School reform is a social challenge, not a technological problem.

Instead, much credit goes to a new quality in human relationships. "Visitors to these schools," the report notes, "quickly sense that teachers and other staff members genuinely love and care for the students. . . The improvements in student behavior were also influenced by the changes in the extent to which children came to understand that they were valued and respected." In all nine schools, the principals "knew all of the students by name and knew many of the families. The personal relationships among students and school staff created a powerful context for good behavior." At all nine schools, parents too became active, engaged, creative partners. This happened because the schools clearly expressed their need and respect for the parents—and because the parents saw "tangible evidence of the school's concern for their children."

Larry Cuban, professor of education at Stanford University, has documented how U.S. education policymakers have careened from one new technology to the next—lantern slides, tape recorders, movies, radios, overhead projectors, reading kits, language laboratories, televisions, computers, multimedia, and now the Internet—sure each time that they have discovered educational gold. Eventually, the glimmer always fades, and we find ourselves holding a lump of pyrite—fool's gold.

Perhaps what we're looking for is not a technology, not a product to be bought and sold at all. Perhaps the gold is something to be mined and refined within ourselves.

Could it be that simple, and that hard?

Some of the world's most thoughtful teachers have suggested as much. John Dewey spoke of the eight loves that mark great teachers—love of others, love of being with children, love of knowledge, of communicating knowledge, of a particular subject that one has an aptitude for, and love of arousing in others similar intellectual interests, a love of thinking, and the ability to inspire in others one's own love for learning itself.

And Rudolf Steiner, the Austrian innovator, advised, "Accept the children with reverence. Educate them with love. Send them forth in freedom."

Those who place their faith in technology to solve the problems of education should look more deeply into the needs of children. The renewal of education requires personal attention to students from good teachers and active parents, strongly supported by their communities. It requires commitment to developmentally appropriate education and to the full range of children's real low-tech needs—physical, emotional, and social, as well as cognitive.

Massachusetts Institute of Technology (M.I.T.) Professor Sherry Turkle has asked: "Are we using computer technology not because it teaches best but because we have lost the political will to fund education adequately?" Her question deserves an answer.

In view of the overwhelming evidence summarized here and the urgent needs of our children and schools, the Alliance for Childhood calls for the following actions:

Recommendations

1. A refocusing in education, at home and school, on the essentials of a healthy childhood: strong bonds with caring adults; time for spontaneous, creative play; a curriculum rich in music and the other arts; reading books aloud; storytelling and poetry; rhythm and movement; cooking, building things, and other handcrafts, and gardening and other hands-on experiences of nature and the physical world.

2. A broad public dialogue on how emphasizing computers is affecting the real needs of children, especially children in low-income families.

3. A comprehensive report by the U.S. Surgeon General on the full extent of physical, emotional, and other developmental hazards computers pose to children.

4. Full disclosure by information-technology companies about the physical hazards to children of using their products.

5. A halt to the commercial hyping of harmful or useless technology for children.

6. A new emphasis on ethics, responsibility, and critical thinking in teaching older students about the personal and social effects of technology.

7. An immediate moratorium on the further introduction of computers in early childhood and elementary education, except for special cases of students with disabilities. Such a time-out is necessary to create the climate for the above recommendations to take place.

9

Computer Literacy Is Vital to Students' Future Success

Diane Rezendes Khirallah

Diane Rezendes Khirallah is the senior editor of Information Week *magazine.*

Less than half of America's children have access to the Internet. The "digital divide" between technology "haves" and "have-nots" is a serious problem for the nation's schools, many of which cannot afford computer technology. The digital divide is also a serious concern for corporate America, which currently suffers from a shortage of information technology (IT) professionals. Some companies have programs designed to help disadvantaged schools implement computer-assisted education, but much more needs to be done in order to prepare America's youth for the IT workforce.

Information technology (IT) director Sue Becker wants more. She wants a bigger budget to bring her IT infrastructure up to capacity. She wants more bandwidth for her network. And she could use a couple of additional support staffers so her team can be more responsive to the 120-plus people who rely on her for their technology needs.

Becker isn't an IT manager in a multinational company; her employer is Link Community School in Newark, New Jersey. And when it comes to IT, she is IT: CIO [chief information officer], manager, tech support, help desk, and teacher to the faculty, staff, and 120 sixth-, seventh-, and eighth-grade students at the nondenominational middle school that sits in what was once one of the most devastated areas of Newark—a city that has long struggled with poverty and its share of violence.

When Becker says she has an IT challenge, she's not overstating her case. Aside from six Apple iMacs that came from a grant, Becker characterizes the school's vintage Macs and PCs—most in various states of disrepair—as "a veritable museum." The machines are a hodgepodge of hardware from local businesses and well-intentioned individuals.

And the Internet? "I'm not sure we could even load a browser on these machines," Becker says. The school's one 56-Kbps dial-up connection is so unreliable that E-mail can take as long as a week—when it goes through at all.

The digital divide and America's schools

Like many other schools across the country, Link is firmly ensconced on the far side of the digital divide, the gap between technology "haves" and "have nots," generally measured by access to the Internet. A study released last month [February 2001] by the Pew Internet & American Life Project finds 45% of American children have access to the Internet. Of these 30 million, the study doesn't distinguish between those who wait in line to log on at the library from those in homes with high-speed access. Nearly three-quarters of youngsters between ages 12 and 17 go online; under age 12, that figure drops to 29%.

It's a divide most clearly delineated by three factors: race, geography, and economic status. On the surface, children at inner-city Link meet all the descriptors that mark the divide: 99% of the students are African-American; 1% are Hispanic. Nearly 40% come from families whose gross annual income is less than $14,000, well below the current U.S. poverty level of $17,650 for a family of four. But don't feel sorry for Link. The private school where everyone is on financial assistance is proud to count doctors, attorneys, and Ph.D.s among its 1,500 alumni. Ninety-five percent of its graduates will complete high school, compared with the city norm of 50% and the statewide average of 79.3%. So far, this success hasn't been because of technology; it's been in spite of it.

Corporate IT, safely perched on the tech-rich side of the divide, sees the need to help schools such as Link. An Information Week Research survey of 500 business and IT professionals finds 77% concerned about the divide. A full 63% of respondents say private business should take on a significant role in bridging the technology gap, yet only a third of the respondents' companies have policies or programs to bring computers into the community.

Not surprisingly, survey respondents say the chief concern of business is the continued shortage of IT workers and how it will affect the U.S. economy. Nearly 70% of survey respondents say their companies are concerned about the digital divide because they, and the U.S. economy in general, need more IT talent. Business still has a great need for tech workers, despite a growing talent pool created by recent layoffs. Short-term solutions such as increasing the number of H-1B visas have had little more than a palliative effect. To address the issue requires long-term strategy.

But the average CIO doesn't necessarily have time in a 50- or 60-hour workweek to think about long-term education strategy, says Brown University's Chris Amirault, director of the Institute for Elementary and Secondary Education. Still, to remain competitive in the global economy, he says, "the reality is that [IT executives] must think about how to create a worker class five, 10, 15 years down the road."

Many technology vendors have involved themselves in digital-divide initiatives for some time. But something's changed: Their philanthropic efforts historically have been fueled by a desire to do good in the community and to reap the benefits of tax write-offs; today, they're also fueled by economic necessity, namely educating the future IT workforce. In all, 61% of survey respondents say more computers in the classroom will help bridge the digital divide, the top initiative cited. Computers in community centers (59%) and mandatory computer competency in public schools (55%) follow closely behind.

Corporate digital-divide initiatives

Hewlett-Packard, for its part, wants to attract children to science and engineering and into solid technology careers, and has the digital-divide initiatives to prove it. But it's tough, says HP's Cathy Lipe, manager of pre-university education programs. "The numbers [of kids pursuing engineering] aren't growing, even though the demand is growing," Lipe says. "It's a recruiting issue that's not immediately felt, because we're losing good talent when kids in grades K to 12 aren't getting into the technology pipeline."

The issue is even broader for Cisco Systems, which also has digital-divide initiatives in place. "It's not just the IT workforce," says Christine Hemrick, the networking vendor's VP for strategic policy. "As companies reinvent business processes around technology, virtually every job will require a basic understanding of how IT works," she says. At Cisco, where company benefits information is distributed online, even manufacturing workers must know how to use a browser at a kiosk.

> *The chief concern of business is the continued shortage of IT workers and how it will affect the U.S. economy.*

After hearing Cisco CEO John Chambers speak, Jack Cassidy, CEO of telecommunications and wireless services provider Cincinnati Bell, says he found himself thinking about computers in education. "Education represents two things that are lifeblood" for Cincinnati Bell and other companies, he says. They are future employees and future consumers. That's why Cincinnati Bell is creating a telecom curriculum for Taft High School, so that it can open an IT academy. The academy was born out of a collaboration between the Cincinnati school district and the Greater Cincinnati Chamber of Commerce.

Around the time that Cincinnati public school administrators realized they had to do something drastic to address a 40% to 75% high school dropout rate, the chamber of commerce began a program to transform the area into a high-tech region. So the two groups teamed up to create the IT academy that will offer students an opportunity to acquire skills and certification in IT, telecom, and electronic media. Despite its technology slant, the program isn't vocational; students will attend traditional high school classes, too.

As for the students who will attend Taft's IT academy (many of whom live in nearby projects in the poorest areas of the city), Cincinnati Bell is considering wiring their homes with free digital subscriber lines so they can have Internet access, Cassidy says. Also on the idea board: on-site telecom classes for Taft students at Cincinnati Bell's state-of-the-art data center, company employees as teachers, and internships for the academy's best and brightest.

Though most companies involved in digital-divide initiatives are technology vendors, some nontech companies are providing funds and volunteers. Richard Shellito, VP of systems at State Farm Insurance Co. in Bloomington, Illinois, says the digital divide goes beyond just the lack of computers or Internet access. "Students must also have the analytical and math skills to understand technology," he says.

In addition to participating in a computer-donation program with its communities, the insurance company has established policies to promote technology know-how in disadvantaged areas. Mark Harms, a recruiting and hiring analyst, runs an eight-week summer program designed to integrate technology into schools and to meet state education objectives. Two teachers and 13 students meet at company headquarters each year. In 2000, the effort resulted in TeacherOutreach.org, an online resource for teachers about using software and the Internet. Created by a handful of people, it's now used by 1,100 Illinois teachers.

Bridging the cultural divide

There's another divide that's harder to measure than socioeconomic status, geography, and race: the cultural chasm between business and education. Without bridging that cultural gap, good intentions, and even tightly focused, well-funded programs, may miss the mark. CIOs have long known that they can't just throw money at IT and expect it to succeed. Similarly, companies can't throw money—or hardware and software—at schools, hoping that somehow the technology will catch on.

The business milieu is one that involves clear outcomes, measurable goals, and specific, agreed-to standards: Money is its driver. But schools aren't in business to turn a profit. Their culture is hard for businesses to grasp, says Brown's Amirault. "We haven't done a good job of explaining why people should use technology. Job preparedness is a lame explanation," he says. "Teachers aren't buying it. Schools aren't set up to embrace technology the way corporations are."

Companies can't throw money—or hardware and software—at schools, hoping that somehow the technology will catch on.

Eric Hartwig, principal at Menlo-Atherton High School in Menlo Park, California, agrees that companies need to understand the culture of education. "It's easy to say, 'Schools should behave as businesses.' But we don't have the structure or the liberty to act as businesses," he says.

Hartwig's school draws students out of five communities, from Menlo-Atherton to East Palo Alto, which has the highest dropout rate in the San Francisco Bay area. The school is proud of its ethnic diversity: Caucasians, African-Americans, Latinos, Asians, and Pacific Islanders make up the student body, and there's no ethnic majority. Some come from homes where the technology includes T1 lines and personal tech support from parents who are IT executives. At the other extreme are students with no PC at home and working parents to whom the Internet remains a mystery.

Step into Manuel Delgado's class in computer basics, and it's quiet except for the tikka-tikk-tikka of 30 sets of hands working 30 keyboards. Delgado says a lot of his students don't have PCs at home, so they need to increase their skills at school. For some, this course will serve as the foundation for programming courses; for others, it's a good basis for college or for entry-level jobs after graduation.

The challenge to corporate philanthropy is . . . to forge partnerships with education. . . . The future IT workforce, and the strength of the nation's economy, may depend on it.

Where do Menlo-Atherton's computers come from? A variety of sources, including the school budget, donations, grants, fund-raisers, and lobbying by parents who are Silicon Valley heavyweights who want more technology in the school.

On the surface, Menlo-Atherton would seem a good fit for Cisco's Networking Academy, which was highly publicized when it was launched in 1997. Initially created to train teachers and students to maintain their schools' IT infrastructures, the program has evolved into an in-depth curriculum leading to student certification in Cisco networking and a near-guarantee of IT employment.

The Networking Academy is also Cisco's top digital-divide initiative. "It's great for students at risk and schools in [federally designated] empowerment zones," says Susan Jeannero, senior manager of education marketing. And it's close to Cisco's core values. "Education is always top of mind. An educated workforce is critical to adapt to the Internet economy." In addition to schools, Cisco offers the program in community colleges, adult learning centers, juvenile detention centers, and even homeless shelters.

Still, Menlo-Atherton decided not to continue with Cisco's Networking Academy after using it for a year. The vendor's offer, which included hardware, teacher training, and a two-year curriculum, was "very sexy, but not as successful as we'd hoped," principal Hartwig says. "From an IT point of view, it's very accessible, but the curriculum is more sophisticated than a lot of kids are ready to handle."

That's not to say he thinks it couldn't work. Hartwig would like to see the IT industry get more involved with implementation; in Cisco's case, to release an employee for a year to work in the schools. "That person could become familiar with adolescent learning and psychology, and learn how the school system actually works," he says.

In some of the poorest neighborhoods, where schools often lack computers, there are other ways for students to get their hands on technology, thanks to after-school programs such as those supported by San Francisco startup Salesforce.com Inc. through its foundation, Salesforce.com/ foundation.

Launched in December 1999 with an initial $2.5 million of Salesforce founder Marc Benioff's personal funds just two months after the company was born, the foundation supports 14 community technology centers at schools, after-school centers, a YMCA, and even a residential detention center for teens. Benioff says his company works hard to leverage its partnerships: Gateway Inc. provides the hardware, Cisco the networking equipment, and America Online the Internet access. Secretary of State Colin Powell's PowerUP organization provides the working model and ancillary support. In addition to funding for staff and other center needs, Salesforce volunteers its staff as teachers, mentors, and IT experts.

Benioff explored the idea of corporate philanthropy firsthand while working at Oracle, when CEO Larry Ellison asked him in 1997 to head company efforts to get technology into schools. Suddenly, he was living in two worlds. "I spent half my time in management meetings and half in schools in places like south-central Los Angeles and Washington, D.C.," Benioff says. Meeting Powell especially inspired him. When it came time to launch his own company, Benioff wanted to bring what he learned to his new venture.

Suzanne DiBianca, chief service officer and head of Salesforce.com/ foundation, advocates a partnership approach, in which Salesforce and the schools and community centers collaborate from the beginning. "Be up-front about the partnership and how deeply you want to be involved," she advises. "And choose organizations that have great visions for what they would do with the money."

One such group is Community Bridges Beacon, a community technology center housed at Everett Middle School in San Francisco's economically disadvantaged Mission district. The center attracts dozens of neighborhood children and teens after school each day for classes, to do homework, or just to have fun.

Because the most sophisticated IT infrastructure in the world is useless without people who know how to use it, Salesforce.com/foundation requires organizations that receive funds to use at least three-fifths of the money, typically $30,000 of $50,000, to hire qualified staff. IT employees also volunteer in the community centers.

In Salesforce's first six months, its staff put in 500 hours of community service; DiBianca says she hopes to double that this year. The executive team is behind it, she says, and it's good for morale and employee retention.

Many companies want to be generous. Pragmatically, they hope to redress the IT labor shortage that will likely continue for years. Employees also like working for a company that extends its core values of innovation, intellect, and invention into the community. But despite the efforts of contributors across the country, many schools still struggle against big odds, and sometimes, the computers in the classroom come from unexpected places.

Remember the six iMacs at Link Community School? They came from the "have" side of the digital divide, but corporate America had nothing to do with it. It was a student project by 17-year-old Tiffany Halo, a senior at Morristown-Beard Prep School. With guidance from her parents, she started a foundation called the Students Urban Renewal Fund, raised $5,000, got a matching grant from the Victoria Foundation, which awards grants to address the needs of the Newark community, and gave the money to Link for the iMacs.

Now, in part because of Halo's project, the school will standardize its student hardware on the Macintosh platform. It's a start. IT director Becker's $256,000 technology plan for Link calls for a LAN and Internet access, a state-of-the-art technology learning center, and the creation of an interactive Web site. In her ideal world, the entire building would be wired and each classroom would have Internet access. "I want them to have computers so badly," she says. "It's all about the money."

For forward-thinking companies—technology and otherwise—the money is the easy part. The challenge to corporate philanthropy is tougher: to forge partnerships with education in order to transform the digital divide into digital opportunity for all children. The future IT workforce, and the strength of the nation's economy, may depend on it.

10

Traditional Literacy Is More Important than Computer Literacy to Students' Future Success

Susan B. Barnes

Susan B. Barnes is the associate chair and an assistant professor in the Department of Communication and Media Studies at Fordham University.

Functional literacy is much more than just the ability to read and write, or even to access information. In modern society, functional literacy requires a broad range of skills, the most important of which is traditional print literacy, followed by general computer literacy (the ability to use a computer), and culminating in the ability to sort through and process the wealth of information on the Internet, on television, and in other media. Schools should have traditional print-based literacy as their primary goal, and should not overwhelm students with the higher levels of literacy until this primary goal is met. The more that computer literacy is stressed at the expense of traditional literacy in America's classrooms, the greater will be the level of illiteracy in the general population.

In the *Technological Society*, Jacques Ellul argues that education "is becoming oriented toward the specialized end of producing technicians." Today, American educators are being encouraged to follow this trend. Documents such as *Technology for America's Economic Growth*, distributed by the Clinton/Gore Administration, argue for the development of an educational system that teaches technology skills for an information economy. As we move toward the new millennium, educators are encouraged to become wired and turn their schools into nodes on the Internet.

Government and industry alike are pressuring educational institutions to adopt the computer as an educational medium. Although calls for instruction suitable for an information society continue to be heard,

Susan B. Barnes, "Education and Technology: A Cultural Faustian Bargain," *Bulletin of Science, Technology & Society*, vol. 19, February 1999, p. 11. Copyright © 1999 by Sage Publications, Inc. Reproduced by permission.

efforts to construct and use educational software have proven disappointing, and instruction in computer literacy has not yet merited a place beside basic literacy skills. In short, computers have yet to be easily integrated into the curriculum. Still, proponents of computer technology, including Nicholas Negroponte and Seymour Papert, argue that computers are an educational medium that is superior to print-based media.

Technology critic Neil Postman, however, reminds us that similar utopian claims were made on behalf of television. Given television's failure as an educational medium, Postman clarifies the need to critically examine the educational implications of computers. In his book *The End of Education,* Postman states that *"All technological change is a Faustian bargain. For every advantage a new technology offers, there is always a corresponding disadvantage."* This article will discuss some of the advantages and the corresponding disadvantages that computer technology introduces into education, and their cultural implications for educational policy.

Advantages and disadvantages of computers

First, a benefit of the computer is its ability to store information in a binary digital format but display it back to the user in a variety of multimedia styles. In *Being Digital,* Negroponte uses the word digital to emphasize the difference between media that are physically created with atoms (such as books, magazines, and videotape) and media that use the computer's digital bits to store, retrieve, and access information. From this perspective, digital media appear to make Marshall McLuhan's statement that "the medium is the message" irrelevant. Educators do not need to worry about the biases embedded in digital media because they can simulate any medium. This raises the following question: Do digital media imply that the message is the message and the medium is irrelevant?

> *"For every advantage a new technology offers, there is always a corresponding disadvantage."*

Currently, research being conducted at Negroponte's Media Lab is theoretically grounded in this anti-McLuhan premise. For example, Gloriana Davenport's Elastic Media project is attempting to reconfigure analog film into digital formats without considering the biases embedded in the medium. Her project explores bringing the advantages of digital random access to film clips by letting users interactively select digital movies, just as they can randomly choose text-oriented data stored on their computer hard disks.

Traditionally, film is presented in time as a fixed linear medium that expresses a point of view. Essential to the film experience is the ethics of film—the quality and shape of the relationships between filmmaker, subject, artwork, and audience. However, when film is stored as arbitrary digital segments, these relationships do not exist. Viewers must now edit their own version of the film and assume the role of filmmaker by selecting various scenes and connecting them together to make meaningful relationships. What is gained with computer technology is the ability to interactively select digital film segments. But what is now missing is the fixed structure of the film's composition that communicates a message to the viewer. Simply stated, by eliminating the fixed linear structure, the message disappears.

In contrast to the Media Lab's anti-McLuhan position, they are actually supporting his thesis that the medium is the message. When a filmmaker edits visual, verbal, and sound elements into a linear arrangement, a point of view is expressed. Conversely, when the elements are unconnected and left for the viewer to arrange, the point of view is eliminated. Whereas digital media make it easier to select and assemble movie elements in a variety of different ways, they undermine the linear structure of message presentation. This is the first example of technology's Faustian bargain at work.

Second, educational computer proponents, S. Papert and Negroponte, argue that learning by interacting with computer-simulated models is superior to learning by reading a book. This argument is reminiscent of John Dewey's argument that learning through experience is the best method of education. Papert argues that the computer supports experiential learning and problem solving. Therefore, computers enhance the learning process. However, in Papert's work the real world is replaced by the microworld of computer simulation. Although there is something to be said for training and instruction using computerized virtual reality, there is always a question as to whether the simulation is an accurate model of the phenomenon represented. Whereas simulation can aid in the understanding of complex scientific concepts, it cannot replace experiences with nature and the real world.

In Papert's vision for the future of education, he wants to replace abstract print-based media with concrete computer-based media. He argues against the printed book because educators have a tendency to overvalue abstract reasoning. Papert asserts that abstract reasoning is a major obstacle to progress in education. But in his vision of education, Papert fails to realize that the computer is an abstract medium. Specifically, he neglects to understand that children who experience the world through computer-generated constructions are actually learning in an abstract, not a concrete, environment. This point is argued in detail by Steve Talbott in his book *The Future Does Not Compute*. Talbott states that

> It is true that the computer is a concrete object—a magnet focal point around which the schoolchild may happily revolve. It is also true that we can, if we choose, assimilate innumerable learning activities to the computer, interest the child in them, and thereby enable him to learn "concretely."

But Papert has a strange definition of concrete that stresses student involvement without looking at what it is the student is involved *with*. Computers themselves are concrete objects. Beyond that, they host a mediated and abstract world. Although computers may be a more physically interactive medium than a book, they add another level of abstraction to the learning process because students are working with simulated rather than real objects. Whereas we gain interactivity, we simultaneously lose touch with the real world. Here again is the Faustian bargain at work.

Third, computer educators argue that hypertext, such as the World

Wide Web, empowers students because they have access to a far wider range of background and contextual materials that are not possible with conventional printed books. Hypertext's ability to connect various pieces of information makes it a valuable scholarly tool for the collection and dissemination of texts. By freeing the text from the static confines of print, hypertext provides students with an interactive, individualized, student-centered learning tool that they can explore without the direct guidance of a teacher. According to B.P. Landow, "Students making use of hypertext systems participate actively in two related ways: they act as reader-authors both by choosing individual paths through linked primary and secondary texts and by adding texts and links to the [hypertext itself]."

Computers add additional levels of literacy skills to traditional skills, and when people discover this they will not want to take the time to become literate.

Similarly, hypertext writing demands additional active collaboration between student and teacher and between student and student. This collaborative use of texts is not possible in the world of print technology. As a result, G. Barrett argues that the active participation of hypertext readers-writers creates a new form of social interaction that turns hypertext into a "sociomedia." He states that hypertext "forces us to look outward from the machine into the complex interaction of human relationships which define 'education.'" Along the same lines, Stephanie Gibson argues that hypertext, when properly used, has the potential to undermine hierarchical relationships between student and teacher, and student and textbook. As a result, hypertext makes education more democratic.

However, it should be noted that the hierarchical and linear organization of knowledge is a key characteristic of current print-based education. Although potentially democratizing education, hypertext simultaneously destroys the print-based organization of knowledge. Teaching children to understand the orderly unfolding of a plot or a logical argument is a crucial part of contemporary education. The presentation of broken hypertexts erodes the deep structures embedded in linear literate modes of communication. In this sense, hypertext may reinforce and accentuate television's tendency toward discontinuity and incoherence.

Furthermore, educators who are introducing hypertext into the classroom have noticed that users get lost. The same hypertext program that allows a search through vast amounts of material has the propensity to lose the user in hyperspace. Students frequently do not know where they are, how they got there, and how to find the information they are looking for. As a result, hypertext may contribute to the electronic media's tendency to overload us with information, which in turn leads to a sense of impotence.

Technology and literacy gap

An additional argument against hypertext is the fact that it further technologizes the word, creating a huge social gap between techno-literates and techno-illiterates, between those who can ride the technological wave to financial rewards and those who must remain outside its direct influence. Gerald M. Phillips, in an essay entitled "A Nightmare Scenario: Literacy & Technology," asserts that

> In a world where technology and literacy marry, we can expect to see an increase in functional illiteracy. There are estimates that as many [as] 40% of the people in our society are currently functionally illiterate. The equivocal phrase appears to mean that people watch too much television and do not read so many books. We can expect functional illiteracy to rise when people discover what technology skills they must master to cope with the world in which they will live.

Whereas Postman asserts that television "amuses us to death," Phillips argues that computer technology is "overwhelming us." Computers add additional levels of literacy skills to traditional skills, and when people discover this they will not want to take the time to become literate. G.M. Phillips also points out that "whatever glowing words are said about the wonders of computer communication . . . the bottom line is that the computer is a literate and linear machine. It employs binary mathematics and depends on grammar. When humans fail to follow the rules, the machine does not respond correctly." Knowledge of these rules is the essence of computer literacy. In 1982, the Association for Computing Machinery listed the following as requirements for teachers to be considered computer literate:

- be able to read and write a simple program,
- have experience using educational software and manuals,
- have a working knowledge of computer terminology,
- be able to discuss the history of computers, and
- be able to discuss the moral or human impact issues.

Now, 15 years after the introduction of computers in education, this definition has changed. According to Papert, computer literacy has come to be defined as a very minimal practical knowledge about computers. Today, we tend to consider anyone who can turn on a computer and access a word processing program to be computer literate. But this is simply not the case, no more than knowing how to use a remote control device means that we understand how a television program is produced and how shots and scenes are combined to produce significant messages. True computer literacy, knowledge of the rules of computing and programming, is a source of power in an information society. The social gap between techno-literates and techno-illiterates ultimately is a power gap as well, one that seems likely to favor economic and social stratification.

Lost in the techno-rhetoric of the information highway is a basic understanding of literacy.

Although hypertext proponents argue that computers democratize education, hypertext does not support linear and literate methods of thinking that are a foundation for computer literacy. Consequently, re-

placing print-based media with computer media could create a major social literacy gap. This is the final and most significant Faustian bargain
that we could make with computers.

Cultural implications

Educators have mixed reactions to the introduction of computers into education. One reason is because they are aware that "each medium has its
own profile of cognitive advantages and disadvantages, and each medium
can be used to enhance the impact of the others. In short, to return to Marshall McLuhan, each medium has its own message." Before we replace traditional educational media with computers, we should better understand
the advantages and disadvantages of computer-mediated environments. To
avoid entering into a Faustian bargain with computers, educators need to
ask the simple question: Why? Why is the computer a better medium?
What advantages does it bring to the learning process? In many cases, we
may be surprised to learn that the answer is it is *not* a better educational
medium. Moreover, the disadvantages may counter the advantages.

But asking these questions is only the beginning. More important, educators need to examine the rhetoric and assumptions of government
policies toward technology and education. In the United States, government and industry are encouraging educators to integrate computing into
the curriculum by donating machines, setting up grant programs, and
asking schools to connect to the Internet. The goal is to focus on developing high-tech literacy for an information economy. [Former president]
Bill Clinton said the following in his State of the Union Address:

> Tenth, we must bring the power of the Information Age
> into all our schools. I challenged America to connect every
> classroom and library to the Internet by the year 2000, so
> that, for the first time in history, a child in the most isolated
> rural town, the most comfortable suburb, the poorest inner-
> city school will have the same access to the same universe
> of knowledge. I ask your support to complete this historic
> mission.

Bringing the Information Age into all our schools by connecting classrooms to the information highway makes an assumption about the nature
of education. The information highway metaphor (promoted by [former]
Vice President Al Gore) implies moving information from one place to another. When applied to education, however, it seems to assume that access
to information *is* education. More and more, this notion is filtering into educational discourse. There seems to be a growing misunderstanding between delivering a message and the goals of teaching and learning. Send-
ing the same message to every classroom in America does not mean that
every student will be able to understand it. Although a first-, second-, or
third-grade student will be able to click on an icon with a mouse and access
information, reading and comprehending the information requires traditional literacy skills. Mastery of traditional literacy skills creates a power balance in computer-mediated communication. Danny Goodman states that

Even if the most compelling applications should become

available at no or low cost tomorrow, there would still be a significant division between the literate and illiterate members of our society. These groups, in my opinion, are the true "haves" and "have-nots" on the information superhighway. If a person can't read text that comes down the off-ramp, then it's not text or information: it's visual noise.

Lost in the techno-rhetoric of the information highway is a basic understanding of literacy. Somehow the concept of information access overshadows the reality that there are estimates that 40% to 50% of the American population is currently illiterate. By the year 2000, everyone may have access to the Internet. But how many people will be able to read the information? Moreover, how many will be able to understand it?

In contrast to the American approach to literacy is a Canadian perspective. The following is a quote from Joyce Fairbairn, a Canadian minister with special responsibility for literacy:

> There is no one right goal for our literacy activities. As a minister, it is my responsibility to make every effort to convince Canadians of the value of literacy and of the importance of our efforts to improve Canadians' literacy skills. We must speak of personal development and of the many ways that literacy enriches our lives. We must speak about how literacy enables citizens to participate fully and productively in their society and government. We must speak of how we are building a learning society where people need better skills to deal with technological change and to gain access to jobs in service industries that rely on Canadians' creativity and analytical skills. Our learning society requires Canadians not only to read, but to read well.

A difference between the American approach and this Canadian perspective is the focus of the educational effort. Americans rely on technology to solve their literacy problem; conversely, this Canadian minister wants to count on people. Not all Americans agree with the president's proposal. For example, Tom Harrison, a California seventh- and eighth-grade teacher, argues against Clinton's view of the Internet. Harrison makes the following statement in the June 1997 issue of *Computers & Society*:

> Even if computer/Internet literacy was a mandate, the correct curriculum path would not be Internet first. It might be something like: Reading/writing literacy, typing/keyboarding/general computer literacy, a variety of computer application programs, computer mechanics and ethics—*then* the Internet.

Literacy in the information society is the most complex form of literacy we have ever known because it adds additional levels of computer literacy skills to traditional skills. For example, in addition to traditional writing skills, journalists working on World Wide Web sites need to be graphic designers and HTML (hypertext mark up language) programmers. Learning these additional skills is very time consuming and many of them have not been fully integrated into the curriculum. Moreover, the relationship between technology and literacy has not been carefully examined. In the United States, access to information seems to be equated with being literate. But this is simply not the case.

Phillips's description of a nightmare scenario for the future of literacy becomes even darker when we look at the World Wide Web. Web designers are adding more television-like features to the Internet. In the past, educators have fought to keep television out of the classroom. Today, many American educators do not seem to realize that the Web is becoming television! Clinton's proposal puts a television-oriented medium directly in schools and the classroom. A future of Web-based learning through the Internet and PC-TVs does not look good for improving the declining literacy skills in the United States. Replacing textbooks with the World Wide Web could amuse some students and overwhelm others.

The literacy gap

We need to examine the possible consequences of replacing traditional print-based learning tools with computers in all aspects of education, including the classroom, the home, and distance learning through the Internet. Although the Internet attempts to equalize access to information, focusing on access rather than actual literacy issues could further the problem of illiteracy in the United States and elsewhere. Instead of making education more democratic, computers could widen the gap between people who are technologically literate and those who are completely illiterate.

11

Computer-Assisted Education Could Radically Alter the Role of Teachers

Frederick Bennett

Frederick Bennett is a retired psychologist and the author of Computers as Tutors: Solving the Crisis in Education.

On a national level, computer-assisted education has failed to produce substantial improvements in students' academic performance—but this is because schools have not allowed students to interact with computers effectively. The power of computers to educate lies in their interactivity and ability to absorb students' attention. But in traditional classrooms, teachers and other students make direct student-computer interaction impossible. In effective computerized education, computers would serve as tutors that teach students directly. Teachers would not become obsolete, but the teacher's role would shift from instructor to "leader teacher" who would be responsible for leading children as they pursue computer-based education.

In a piece published in February 2001, syndicated columnist George Will used Hippocrates and Socrates to illustrate the difficulties in contemporary American schooling. "If you were ill and could miraculously be treated by Hippocrates or by a young graduate of Johns Hopkins medical school, with his modern technologies and techniques, you would choose the latter. But if you could choose to have your child taught either by Socrates or by a freshly minted holder of a degree in education, full of the latest pedagogical theories and techniques? Socrates, please."

Teaching has always been more art than science and depends heavily on the talents of the practitioner. Some teachers are outstanding; some are not. In medicine, Hippocrates probably had more innate abilities than many of the new physicians, but his successors have the advantage of modern technology. Teachers, however, rely on basically the same approach that instructors have used throughout history, and, consequently,

Frederick Bennett, "The Future of Computer Technology in K–12 Education," *Phi Delta Kappan*, vol. 83, April 2002, p. 621. Copyright © 2002 by Phi Delta Kappa, Inc. Reproduced by permission.

they must count on their own native skills. This situation presents a difficulty for education because exceptional instructors are in the minority. We see this easily if we think back over the teachers that we ourselves had in our school career. The number we remember as superb is not large.

The present

Education today, as always, depends on the luck of the draw—who gets the good teachers and who gets the others. Meanwhile, technology has become a powerful force in the world. Theoretically, it might change education, just as it has made the new physician better equipped than Hippocrates and has brought dazzling benefits to innumerable other areas of society. Education authorities apparently hoped for comparable results because they have placed millions of computers in schools. By 1999, there was one computer for every six children. Yet despite this massive infusion of technology, overall improvements in education have been minimal.

Scores on the National Assessment of Educational Progress point up this lack of advancement. Results for 1999 showed no significant change in reading, mathematics, or science for the three age groups tested—9-year-olds, 13-year-olds, and 17-year-olds—from 1994 through 1999. During this five-year period, schools acquired huge numbers of computers and hoped earnestly that this influx of technology would improve education.

Since few people want to despair and conclude that K-12 education seems to be about the only major field that technology cannot benefit, authorities have sought reasons for the current failure. The most frequently suggested explanation is that teachers have not learned how to employ technology in their classrooms. Therefore, if schools could train teachers, the argument goes, technology would finally deliver major benefits to education. Former President Bill Clinton joined those who wanted additional teacher training when in June 2000 he announced $128 million in grants to instruct teachers in the use of technology.

We could allow computers to tutor children individually and directly, without a teacher in the usual role.

Lack of teacher training, however, is a myth. In 2000 the U.S. Department of Education issued a study in which half of all teachers reported that college and graduate work had prepared them to use technology. In addition, training continues after formal schooling. The same government document pointed out that, from 1996 to 1999, 77% of teachers participated in "professional development activities in the use of computers or the Internet." Thirty-three percent to 39% of teachers responding to two surveys in 1999 said that they felt well prepared to use computers. Although not the full universe of teachers, this percentage of well-prepared instructors ought to have brought some improvement if technology were going to lift education to a higher plateau.

The failure of test scores to change after schools have added millions of computers, after teachers have received considerable training, and after many years of computer usage leads to a troubling question: Is it possible that technology as currently used can never fundamentally improve today's K–12 education? I believe that such hopelessness is indeed warranted, for one obvious reason: the power of electronic interaction is necessarily diminished because of the way computers must be used in schools today.

Interaction takes place when the instructor and the student react directly to each other's contributions. Interaction between child and teacher has always been found in good instruction. It can make learning enjoyable, can adjust to the varied abilities of different students, and is effective with children of all ages. Very possibly, one of the attributes of the teachers that we remember as being superb was their ability to develop a high degree of interaction with us.

Computer games show the power of electronic interaction. The secret to a large portion of this technology's success in maintaining its iron grip on the attention of game players is the unparalleled ability of the machine to interact continually with the participant. Theoretically, this same interactive power ought to make computers a potent force in education. When computers are used in classrooms today, however, interaction between the computer and the student cannot be strong and ongoing. This is because the teacher, not the computer, must control and direct instruction. Individual teachers must decide how they will use computer instruction in the dissemination of classroom material—how much the machine will teach the student and how much instruction the teacher will provide. These conditions are unalterable in the present system of education, and they drastically curtail interaction between the computer and the student.

Business and computers

American education, however, is not unique in its poor initial results with computers. Corporate America had a similar experience. For several years, businesses added large numbers of computers, but overall productivity did not improve. Many workers acquired the machines for their desks. They used them for important jobs such as word processing and spreadsheets, but the basic manner in which companies carried on their activities did not change. This kind of computer usage was bound to fail. In time, corporations made the necessary structural changes and thus altered the basic way they carried on their business. When that happened, productivity increased dramatically. In an extensive article about the increase in productivity that technology has brought to business, Erik Brynjolfsson and Lorin Hitt point out, "Investments in computers may make little direct contribution to overall performance of a firm or the economy until they are combined with complementary investments in work practices, human capital, and firm restructuring."

Education is in a position today akin to that of American business in those early days. Despite the millions of computers in schools, teaching has not changed. In the encompassing evaluation of technology in schools mentioned above, the Department of Education notes, "According to the literature, the advent of computers and the Internet has not dramatically changed how teachers teach and how students learn."

An alternative

There is an alternative to the way we use computers in schools, an alternative that would take advantage of the power of interaction. We could allow computers to tutor children individually and directly, without a teacher in the usual role. This approach seems radical when first considered. Nonetheless, a few schools have tried it for some students or subjects. The usual students in these computerized classes are those who are at risk of dropping out of school. In many cases, these students have been so difficult to teach that authorities have allowed this new approach. The results have been uniformly good.

Several companies have developed fitting teaching software. Among these are Plato Learning, Inc., Scientific Learning, and NovaNet Learning, Inc. All three have Web pages on which the results of their programs are posted.

Lakeland High School in Florida, Lawrence High School in Indianapolis, and Turner High School in Carrollton, Texas, provide three interesting examples of Plato programs. In retests in Lakeland, student FHSCT (Florida High School Competency Test) scores increased dramatically, and the school identified a significant positive relationship between some Plato student performance data and the FHSCT scores. Authorities at Lawrence implemented an extensive remediation program in 1998–99 to increase the passing rate of their students taking the state-mandated competency exam, ISTEP (Indiana Statewide Testing for Educational Progress). At the beginning of the year, 406 students failed either the math or the English component. At the end of the year, only 74 of those pupils continued to fail the exam. At Turner, the pass rate on TAAS (Texas Assessment of Academic Skills) reversed a trend and improved from 69% in 1998 to 83% in 2000.

The electronic instructor could be programmed to emulate the approaches that good teachers have always used with their students.

Scientific Learning has concentrated on reading and comprehension, especially with students who are behind in these vital areas. Pretest and posttest results with standardized, nationally normed tests showed significant gains with various levels of students from kindergarten through grade 12.

Dillard High School in Fort Lauderdale, Florida, provides an example of the results of using NovaNet software. In this program there were 123 students, all of whom were below the 20th percentile on state standards. After three months of using the program, all pupils had made gains. Moreover, half of the students had advanced at least one full grade, and 27 of those pupils had improved by either two or three grade levels.

Although schools have used this form of computerized education primarily with at-risk children, there are other programs that teach average and bright students, and they have recorded equally exciting gains. For example, researchers at Carnegie Mellon University created software to teach algebra through computers. They installed the program in a number of high schools, including some in their hometown of Pittsburgh. The authors made a study of freshmen at three schools, none of whom had taken the subject in middle school. Approximately 470 students enrolled in 21 computer classes. At the end of the year the schools assessed results and compared math achievement for these students with that of a comparable group of 170 ninth-grade students in standard math courses. The results showed the power of the computerized learning. The computer students scored 15% better on standardized tests. Moreover, they scored 100% better on the more difficult questions that "focused on mathematical analysis of real-world situations and the use of computational tools."

[A] vitally important activity for humans in the education of children would be to function as leader teachers.

In all these successful programs the electronic instruction takes advantage of many of the strengths of computers: children are taught individually and at their own pace, and the software develops interaction between the computer and the student. Moreover, the electronic instructor never retires or gets sick, and programmers can continually improve the software. Teachers continue to be essential, but with a role that differs from our accustomed conception of what teachers do.

Careful consideration of results from these and other studies makes it seem possible that, if this type of computerized education were adopted universally, technology could begin to make real and beneficial changes for students, teachers, and schools. Under this scenario, not only would there be interaction between the computer and the student, but also each pupil would have, in effect, a private tutor throughout his or her educational career. Like a human tutor, the electronic instructor would teach the child at his or her learning level. For example, superior students would constantly have new vistas and challenges opened to them, with continual opportunities for advancement. With sub-par students, the computer would provide appropriate material but would also move at a speed that would fit each pupil's capacity for progress.

Through constant testing and continual interaction, the electronic instructor would be aware of the child's needs and would immediately provide proper material to correct any problems and to encourage and help the student to advance. Students who had more difficulty learning would never be overwhelmed because the class had proceeded beyond their level of scholarship. Moreover, there would be no embarrassment if the computer had to take longer to cover a given lesson for a particular student. The child's classmates would not know. Only the computer and the authorities receiving the computer reports would have this information. At the other end of the learning spectrum, students who were capable of advancing more rapidly would find new excitement and challenges, and much of the boredom that has always engulfed these students would be removed.

Moreover, the electronic instructor could be programmed to emulate the approaches that good teachers have always used with their students. It would point out errors and praise and reinforce all gains. Positive feedback helps the student and makes learning enjoyable, as all teachers recognize. In a classroom of 15 or 20 students, teachers are often unable to give each student individual encouragement. The computer, however, with only one child to attend to, would always be quick to praise his or her accomplishments. Since the computer would interact directly with the child, it could concentrate its power exclusively on the needs of the individual student without affecting the requirements of other children in the class. They would all have their own private tutors.

Teachers

Computerized education would change the role of teachers but would neither eliminate nor downgrade them. On the contrary, human instructors would remain extremely important but with a radically different focus. This possibility often frightens teachers, but computerization would actually enhance their position. Many of the tedious, boring duties that they must endure today, such as preparing daily lesson plans and correcting tests, would vanish. That would leave them more time to function in their true and essential position as educators. There are two basic roles that I foresee for teachers in computerized education: continuing to conduct group activities and acting as "leader teachers."

Many teachers today conduct a variety of group sessions, such as workshops, seminars, and discussions. In computerized education, these duties would not only continue but would take on more importance than in today's schools. In addition, some aspects of today's group meetings would change. The computer would handle the basic necessities of the assigned curriculum, giving teachers greater freedom to choose topics for a group setting and the prospect of dealing more deeply with those topics than is possible today. Group projects might continue for several class periods or for several days. Despite the length of time used in these activities, the students would not miss any of their computer classes because the computer would begin again exactly where the last lesson ended. Today, teachers usually have all the students from their own classes in their groups and no one else. In computerized education, preset conditions would not determine attendance. Students could choose the workshops that most interested them, and teachers could establish prerequisites for attendance. For a teacher, this type of group would form the ideal teaching environment.

One of the fears sometimes voiced about children learning extensively from computers is that they would lose the valuable human give-and-take that currently happens in classes. In actuality, because of the need for discipline, less interplay among students goes on in today's classrooms than is often imagined. But group sessions in computerized education would provide many legitimate opportunities for student interaction.

Another vitally important activity for humans in the education of children would be to function as leader teachers. Every student at every age level would have a leader teacher whom the pupil and his or her parents would choose and who would be responsible for leading the child as he or she pursued an education. This relationship between student and teacher would last for at least a year at a time and might continue for several years. The student would meet this mentor privately and on a regular basis. These meetings would vary, depending on the age and needs of the child. For example, the leader teacher of a student in the first grade might see and talk with the child several times every day. The leader teacher of a student in high school might meet with the youth only once every couple of weeks if that seemed appropriate.

All children, however, at all age levels would sit down regularly with their teachers, who would have access to their computer records. Time would be available for the instructors to get to know the children well. This system would make directing the education of the children easier and more productive for the teachers and make the children comfortable with this kind of direction. In today's education system, many students go months or even years without meeting privately with a teacher. That could never happen if computers were teaching and leader teachers had both the responsibility of directing children's education and the time to carry out that responsibility.

Parents would have another advantage because a leader teacher directed their child. They would find it easier to arrange parent/teacher conferences. They would need to meet with only one instructor, who would have a thorough knowledge of the student and of all the subjects he or she was studying.

The future

Can schools ever take advantage of true computerized education? When corporate America learned how it could use computers to improve productivity, the central role of the computer in business was assured. The need for improvement in education is present, as even such staunch defenders of today's schools as the Sandia National Laboratories and Gerald Bracey point out. Moreover, everybody would be delighted if there could be additional gains even among today's best schools.

Emulating the successful employment of computers by business, however, is not simple. There are unique difficulties in education. For example, school boards must alleviate the fears of teachers that they will lose their jobs. In addition, since education is much more involved in the political world, proportionately more people must take part in the process of making changes. The numbers of citizens who must become aware of the potential of computerization in education will be larger than in business, where the decision makers are fewer. In corporate America, when software companies developed programs to enhance productivity, individual businesses bought that software because they wanted to improve and did not fear changes. Education, with some exceptions, has a history of resisting serious change. This tendency lessens the incentive for software companies to develop the necessary programming.

The solution, therefore, must be twofold. First, educators, politicians, parents, and concerned citizens must understand how schools can use computers more effectively to improve education and to benefit students and teachers. Second, commercial companies must create suitable software.

These seem to be monstrous tasks, but both are possible. Many teachers, parents, and administrators want improvements and are engaged in an ongoing search for answers. They will need to examine and debate the value of true computerization as they carry out their quest. If these many searchers for improved education decide that computerization can supply an important portion of the answer, then it will be up to the private corporations to do their part. Some of these are already developing programming, as noted above, and they and other companies could turn more of their resources and ingenuity toward developing outstanding and effective educational software. The potential market is huge, and software corporations will produce the programming as soon as they see that education will accept these changes.

Although there are differences in the paths of education and business in developing the use of computerization, there is one major similarity. American business was not able to take advantage of the power of computer technology until many of its basic practices changed. This is equally true in education. Until schools can permit a major alteration in the way teaching is carried on, they must necessarily continue to miss out on the improvement that computer technology can bring.

12

Computers Cannot Replace Teachers

Vivienne Collinson

Vivienne Collinson is a professor at Michigan State University and the author of Reaching Students: Teachers' Ways of Knowing.

Computers can be effective tools for helping students learn academic subjects, but young people will always need human teachers to provide moral guidance and foster intellectual growth and social development. Computers provide students with information, but only teachers can teach children to think critically, discriminate among sources of information, and be creative. Computers certainly cannot help students with the difficult social and moral problems they face.

I nformation technology is changing people's thinking as profoundly as the printing press changed the course of history more than five centuries ago. The advent of information technology, particularly the computer and the World Wide Web, was hailed as having "the potential to revolutionize education and improve learning." Futurists quickly envisioned "virtual schools" where students spend a great deal of time learning from their computer-as-teacher.

This [viewpoint] argues that as student use of computers increases, teachers will be more indispensable than ever to guide the intellectual, social, and moral development of children. To illustrate this position, the article describes intellectual, social, and moral issues that one teacher has faced in a technology-rich, 21st Century School. Her experiences demonstrate why technology cannot replace teachers and exemplify how computers in schools anywhere can be both a blessing and a burden for teachers.

Educating for intellectual, social, and moral development

Goals of education in the United States have changed little over the last 300 years and generally fall into four categories: academic (intellectual),

Vivienne Collinson, "Intellectual, Social, and Moral Development: Why Technology Cannot Replace Teachers," *High School Journal*, vol. 85, October/November 2001, p. 35. Copyright © 2001 by University of North Carolina Press. Reproduced by permission.

vocational (responsibility as a productive citizen), social and civic (social-ization into a democratic society), and personal (self-development). Goals for high schools are no exception. B.L. Wilson and G.B. Rossman noted that the usual mission of high schools is to "challenge and help students to grow intellectually, personally, and socially, [but that] . . . the primary responsibility . . . , is to promote the intellectual growth of . . . students." Intellectual growth was defined as "the ability to reason, to imagine, to value, to decide."

J.I. Goodlad also found that the "cultivation of cognitive abilities is paramount" in secondary schools, but that for some students, academic work "intrudes into the personal and social" aspects of their lives. The literature indicates that adolescence represents a strong growth period in intellectual and social development. As adolescents develop cognitive capacity to reason, think symbolically, make judgments, and engage in formal operations, they also become interested in social relationships and social issues as well as values and moral issues.

As student use of computers increases, teachers will be more indispensable than ever.

Recent constructivist theories of learning help explain the relationship between intellectual and social development of children; that is, social norms and social interactions play a powerful role in all learning, especially in learning to communicate and empathize with others and behave in culturally acceptable ways. Adolescents tend to learn social behaviors and values from role models and from experiences that personally involve them rather than from direct instruction. Thus, in schools, teachers' actions speak louder than words.

The links between intellectual and moral development have been less explored than the intellectual/social connections. On the intellectual side, J. Dewey argued forcefully for active and engaged learning that involves inquiry, insisting that "on the intellectual side we must have judgment." However, he also argued that "the development of character is the end of all school work." Inquiry, judgments, and character all involve values and therefore fall into the realm of moral education. Additionally, all represent a search for knowledge as well as careful thinking and reflection throughout the process. Thus, "teaching, if it is a reflective enterprise, is necessarily an ongoing effort at moral self-improvement. And moral self-improvement is impossible without the continued quest for self-knowledge and the knowledge of others."

Most of a century passed before other psychologists elaborated Dewey's claim that intellectual and moral development require social/emotional learning in order to flourish. For example, D. Goleman elaborated how empathy is particularly important both for successful relationships and for the development of character. In short, "higher-level thinking" such as tolerance, open-mindedness, decision making (judgments), and respect for evidence remains limited if "emotional intelligence" is not learned. [According to Goleman:]

There is an old-fashioned word for the body of skills that emotional intelligence represents: character . . . The bedrock of character is self-discipline . . . Being able to put aside one's self-centered focus and impulses has social benefits: It opens the way to empathy, to real listening, to taking another person's perspective. Empathy . . . leads to caring, altruism, and compassion.

Authors such as N. Noddings have begun to explore the holistic notion of intellectual, social, and moral development of students as it applies to the curriculum. Noddings wondered what a curriculum would be like if it were not limited to 'the cultivation of cognitive abilities,' but instead focused on helping students flourish as human beings in a complex society. Her work has renewed interest in the holistic development of students. The increased awareness is timely, given that information technology is already impacting teachers and its effects are forcing a reexamination of teaching and learning in an "information age" and "knowledge society." As the remainder of this [viewpoint] indicates, widespread access to computer technology in the classroom brings with it a plethora of social and moral issues that teachers have not previously faced. The next section briefly introduces the teacher and the school used to illustrate some current issues.

The teacher and school

Candice (a pseudonym) is an experienced high school teacher with an undergraduate degree in science and a master's degree in technology. She was a participant (N=81) in a national study that included middle and high school teachers of all subject areas and grades. The participants, who represented urban, suburban, and rural schools in each quadrant of the United States, were nominated as exemplary teachers by groups of peers, staff developers, and/or subject specialists in each region. Although any number of the participants' stories could have illustrated this article, Candice was selected because she teaches math and science in a technology-rich school that was built in the 1990s but was especially designed for the 21st century. Candice has a research background in technology and has developed and taught numerous computer courses at the high school and university level. She has served as the director of a school district's technology center and as a participant on both a statewide technology task force and a statewide computer education curriculum writing team.

Computer technology is a wonderful tool for academic subjects, but also one that forces teachers to deal directly with social and moral issues.

Futurist School (a pseudonym), the school where Candice teaches, was equipped from the outset with a 650-station network for a school population of about 1300 students. The network goes throughout the school on seven file servers. This allows teachers and students to log on to an outstanding CD-ROM system in the library from anywhere in the school. The faculty works together to design technology-based curricula. They learned quickly that computer technology is a wonderful tool for academic subjects, but also one that forces teachers to deal directly with social and moral issues. Candice views intellectual, social, and moral development of students holistically. However, the three dimensions are somewhat separated here for ease of illustration.

Computers and intellectual development

Although the United States met its goal to wire all schools by 2000, use of computer-assisted instruction varies widely. Some schools are wired but not yet set up for easy computer use; other classrooms are already equipped with palm pilots for each student. By the end of 1999, 84% of teachers reported having at least one computer available in their classroom and 99% had computers available somewhere in the school. Early studies indicate that teachers are having a variety of difficulties finding time to learn the new technology and/or incorporating it into the curriculum. Only a third of the nation's teachers report feeling prepared to use computers and the Web in their teaching.

When computers were first introduced into schools, numerous authors debated early questions about the effects on education. One known effect of the introduction of new technologies is that they change cultures by altering the way people think about words like "knowledge," "truth," "freedom," and "learning." Television in the United States is a good example of technology changing a culture. According to Neil Postman, "After television, the United States was not America plus television; television gave a new coloration to every political campaign, to every home, to every school, to every church, to every industry."

In the same way that television changed the American culture, people's lives, and their thinking, according to A. De Vaney, "machines forever change relations within the traditional classroom . . . Technology in the classroom is a cognitive, social, and cultural event." A national study indicated that computers in some classrooms are empowering teachers and students to transform parts of the curriculum, change social interactions, and encourage inquiry. [Researchers M.J. Johnson, R. Schwab, and L. Foa write:]

> As teachers move past the early stages of technology adoption, their classroom content tends to move beyond the confines of the textbook and lecture methodologies . . . They tend to use more collaborative and team structures for organizing students . . . Teaching and learning . . . tend to become more holistically integrated, moving away from segregated and isolated subject areas and classrooms.

In Candice's classroom, moving beyond the textbook means making information relevant for students and integrating the two subjects she teaches. For example, she has students undertake a longitudinal outdoor inquiry in science class so they can later use their own data sets to study statistics in her math class. The students could use examples from the textbook, but their own data are more meaningful. In this way, the unit on statistics is not simply another mystifying or irrelevant hurdle for passing math. Instead, the use of students' data acts as a motivator and brings meaning and intellectual understanding to the strengths and limitations of statistics.

Moving beyond mere facts and skills to making information meaningful is important to Candice. She wants to ensure that during a test, students are not reciting information they have memorized or copied simply to pass a test. She knows that longstanding testing practices with their emphasis on scores have encouraged students to cheat. She also knows that her students do not necessarily see cheating as morally wrong.

> Students cheat when they feel like they don't have a chance
> of being successful; otherwise they wouldn't cheat. So I try
> to create a situation where if you cheat, it's not going to get
> you anywhere. For example, if a student can use their lab
> notebook on a chemistry test and the questions on the test
> are geared towards having completed that lab and [having]
> done your complete write-up, then the student who copies
> the lab into their notebook from somebody else's is still not
> going to be able to do the test because they're not going to
> know what the information and the lab report that they
> copied means.

Candice is aware that some students can be seduced by the common idea that "technique of any kind can do our thinking for us." An early example was the "Thinking Mouse" marketed for Macintosh users. Computers can appear to do our thinking for us. They offer unending bits and sources of information, they alert us to spelling and grammatical errors, and they can, superficially at least, enhance students' work by making presentations look neat and attractive. What computers do very well is access, arrange, and store vast amounts of information. However, because "information is not knowledge, and knowledge is not wisdom," students have to be taught that information posted on the Web is not necessarily accurate or widely accepted as true unless it is supported with credible evidence. Computers do not teach children to question, to discriminate among sources of information, to weigh perspectives, to think about consequences, to bring contextual meaning to a situation, to be creative, or to make careful judgments.

Computers in classrooms have also raised the perennial issue of quality versus quantity to a new level. Candice has been involved with assessment at the state level and she is trying to incorporate ideas about standards and quality into her classroom. She discovered that expectations for quality in students' work have to be made explicit to students who can easily mistake quantity for quality when faced with an information glut. Issues of quality are particularly pertinent in Candice's science classes because students work on individual and group projects and have access to almost unlimited information through computers.

> We spend a fair amount of time [in class] talking about
> what [the] standards are for [students'] work . . . really talk-
> ing about what's required and to some extent, you know,
> having the kids also help with what the quality is . . . [Next

year] I'm going to actually teach a class called Scientific Research. We're going to put up various papers and talk about why this one is good and why this one isn't and find the strong pieces in each part and really work on that.

As access to information increases, teachers will have to teach students how to judge the source, relevance, and quality of information. Teachers will also have to set explicit criteria and expectations for quality and then teach students how to judge the quality and presentation of their own work.

Researchers are just beginning to understand that like other cultures, classroom cultures can also "suffer grievously from information glut, information without meaning, [and] information without control mechanisms." The issue of control of information is as necessary in classrooms as it is in other cultures. Just as courts of law determine which information is admissible or inadmissible, other cultures also find control mechanisms to limit, sort, and judge information. For example, in education, "the invention of what is called a curriculum was a logical step toward organizing, limiting, and discriminating among available sources of information."

As access to information increases, teachers will have to teach students how to judge the source, relevance, and quality of information.

Students in Candice's class have very easy access to information through technology. For example, her students must use a symbolic math program in order to do their assignments. For other assignments, they need access to references through the library's CD-ROM system. "At Futurist School, it is impossible for a student to pass their classes without access to the computers." Like other schools, however, Futurist School has had to control student access to the Web, judging some information inappropriate for adolescent students. Nevertheless, lack of information in this school is not a problem. The challenge for Candice is teaching students how to use and control information.

Having worked on a state curriculum writing team, Candice understands the role of curriculum and standards as information control. However, she is also determined to help students learn to think for themselves and to teach them processes that can help them think.

I suppose that eventually I'm going to find myself in a rather interesting bind on working to develop the state standards and what we think kids need to know by tenth grade. And yet my attitude [is one] of not particularly caring whether or not I get through the curriculum if I can teach the kids . . ., the three basic tenets of my classroom. Because that's really what I'm interested in. There is no way that I can teach them everything they need to know, particularly in science where it's changing every moment. My focus is very much on those three issues: How do you ask questions and good questions? How do you look up the an-

swers to those questions? And then how do you generate
more questions based upon what you found out?

Candice gave several humorous examples of how her insistence on
questions has occasionally backfired and how easy access to information
has been a blessing when that occurs. She has often been amused when
students use questions to try to get out of work or slow down the class.

> There is also the age-old ploy of distracting the teacher . . .
> with the questions that waste time. One of the greatest
> things is the computer in the classroom for [dealing with]
> that . . . So when kids ask those distracting questions, in-
> stead of saying, "Come see me after school" or starting to
> explain it, you say, "Go log on, look it up, and tell us what
> the answer is" and you move on. And that student is dis-
> tracted but the rest of us get to continue.

She can almost predict one question when she teaches the standard
parabola. As she explains how parabolas get wider or narrower depending
on the numbers in the equation, a student invariably asks what happens
when you use one million in the equation.

And so you say, "Well, why don't you go put the graph in an equation on the computer? When you have it up on the screen, we'll all take
a look at it to see. Well, that immediately answers that question and it
takes a question that was supposed to be a distracter and turns it into a
learning tool . . . So technology, in my mind, has been a wonderful way
of dealing with that problem and turning it into something that's positive instead of negative."

Social and intellectual development

In addition to the obvious advantages that computer technology introduces to classrooms, computers have revived the thought that technology
can to some extent replace parents and teachers. Television was perhaps
the first noticeable modern technology to "endanger" children's thinking
and replace parents as teachers. Children were spending many hours in
front of the TV but not interacting with the human beings they were seeing. Moreover, they had no adult to challenge the "thinking" the TV was
doing for them and they often acted out at school what they saw on television without making distinctions or judgments between appropriate
and inappropriate behaviors. Children were physically and mentally in-
active while watching TV. Linguistically, they were not talking, playing
with words, planning responses, or fine tuning their language skills. Socially, they were not practicing skills to help them interact productively
with others. Children did not have to learn how to listen to TV speakers
since they could walk away, talk, or do anything else at the same time the
TV was on. Not surprisingly, experts have recently warned of similar
problems concerning computers.

Contrary to the potential social isolation and lack of involvement
that TV and computer technology can encourage, education has traditionally championed the goal of socializing students into a democratic
society. Classrooms by their very nature represent a complex set of social

interactions and opportunities to practice democratic ideals. [W. Waller writes that] "Children and teachers are not disembodied intelligences, not instructing machines and learning machines, but whole human beings tied together in a complex maze of social connections."

The majority of problems that teachers face on a
daily basis are social issues.

The majority of problems that teachers face on a daily basis are social issues that, if not acknowledged, can distract students from their intellectual work. Candice recalled a situation where she had stayed up very late creating a wonderful, creative lesson only to have social problems interfere with its delivery.

> I got to school and the kids hated [the lesson] and it really hurt my feelings because they were . . . actually behaving in a fairly uncharacteristic way for them . . . Well, what I found out was that something had happened to some kid somewhere else, a lot of these kids knew, and they were upset and they were behaving poorly. [It] had nothing to do with my wonderful lesson. And the kids apologized and they asked if we could do the lesson again.

Candice, like so many other secondary school teachers, knows that adolescents' emotions are often very visible and that they are vulnerable because friendships and peer acceptance mean so much to them. She is sympathetic, but at the same time, she insists that learning remain the focus of the classroom. Candice believes that the learning atmosphere of the classroom improves if students are courteous, so she spends considerable time during the first week of classes on "how students are supposed to behave with one another." She insists that "everybody must be polite and must be courteous, must be sensitive to what other people are feeling. If you need something, you need to use please and thank you." She is a firm believer that "if you respect people and . . . you model consistency and respectfulness most of the time—I don't think anybody can do it all of the time—then the students rise to the occasion and they meet those expectations."

One year, social interference with learning became especially difficult as Candice tried to mediate the tension between two strong students and keep the class focused.

> Occasionally the tension between them overwhelmed the rest of the class. And so there was an instance of it really didn't matter what I did. The atmosphere in the classroom was so tense because of the disagreement between these two students that it was impossible for anybody to pay attention to anything but the uncomfortable atmosphere that these two young women were creating.

In addition to dealing with external effects on student learning and mediating personal conflicts, Candice uses anything possible to help motivate disinterested or disruptive students. She once had two girls who, because of discipline problems, were added to her group on a science visit to a forest. They clearly were not keen about the plan. In this case, Candice used intellectual curiosity to dispel a potentially bad social situation.

> It started to rain and I put out a leaf so it caught [the rain] and then held the magnifying glass above it so they could see [the raindrop] change colors . . . And all of a sudden, these two girls who were really anti-being-in-the-woods were absolutely fascinated and before long they were collecting snails and finding salamanders and asking me what this was and asking me what that was. Did I have a plan for how I was going to work with those girls? No. But did I see stuff around me and make it work to my purpose? You bet. And I do a lot of that.

As one method of checking on students' learning and modeling democratic socialization, Candice has her classes do a small self-assessment each Friday: Students name something they did well that week, something they need to work on or need help with, and something she can do to help them be a better student. She responds to their suggestions, most of which she says are reasonable, and has noticed that her willingness to alter procedures or explain why she cannot implement a specific suggestion has relaxed the teacher/student relationship in a positive way.

Thanks to her many years of experience as a teacher, Candice is aware of the variety of social problems adolescents have to handle and she understands that they need the help of adults to listen and to guide. Moreover, she believes that what adolescents need most is love: "I have a pin that I wear that says 'Educating with Love' and that's really my philosophy—is that every child in my classroom is not only worthy of but deserves to be loved." The students at Futurist School are lucky because the adults know them as individuals. No number of computers could help them through the inevitable upsets that occur during adolescence or persist in helping them to be successful.

> It's really pretty unusual for a kid who's feeling out of sorts and is really kind of down and dragging to go an entire day without a teacher noticing that there is something wrong and taking them aside and asking them if there is something they can do to help . . . And if kids are having trouble learning something, most of the time we're able to sit down and listen and get a better handle on what their learning needs are and what some alternative approaches would be towards helping this kid be successful.

Moral development

Not all classroom problems can be solved so easily. As students gain access to and familiarity with computers, some become proficient with computers in ways their teachers might not envision. Many of these new technology-based issues involve values and judgments and are therefore moral/ethical problems.

Eight years ago kids were so grateful to use a computer and not very many . . . had them at home. And so they pretty much did almost nothing wrong . . . They sent messages across the system that would clutter up people's screens and stuff. And it was fairly simple to solve that problem. We just turned off messaging. But now kids have computers at home and they have computers at home that are far more powerful than our computers at school and they know a whole lot more. And there is a certain breed of mostly young men, but there are some young women involved who, I would say, lack a certain amount of morals. And if they can do it, they do it. Just like there are plenty of things that I know I could do, but just because I can do it doesn't mean it's right to do it.

Society needed a new word for unethical uses of computers and coined the term cybercrime. "Cybercrime encompasses a huge number of unpublicized incidents. And unlike much old-fashioned crime, it's on the rise." Teachers are increasingly familiar with the cybercrime of plagiarism. As a high school student in New York explained, "A lot of people download papers and just change the names. There aren't a lot of original papers that get written anymore." Other examples of cybercrime include "four high school students [who] hacked into an Internet server and used stolen credit card numbers in a $200,000 online shopping spree."

Students must be able to count on help from teachers to develop morally as well as intellectually and socially.

Candice noted that "computer discipline" incidents in Futurist School are accelerating just like the national rate. One incident involved "a kid [who] had given her password to another student and they were writing extremely graphic notes to one another about boyfriend problems and things like that." Some students crossed the moral line by harming others, a clear case of "technological progress" not being equivalent to "human progress."

We had one instance where a kid actually wrote a program, or got a program off a network, that would make it look like you were logging on to the network, but instead it captured your sign-on and your password. And then they would go into other people's accounts and either erase their files or leave filth on their accounts.

Other students "figured out how to change the print queues . . . [so] when people print, [their work] goes off to never-never land and their job never gets to a real printer . . . They wait and they wait and they wait and after an hour, it still hasn't printed. And the reason why it hasn't printed is because it hasn't gone to a printer."

Hacking is still limited to a minority of students in Futurist School, but it is a growing problem.

> All of our high schools in our district, and to some degree
> some of the middle schools, are starting to report this type
> of lack of morals computer problem. And so it's a discon-
> certing type of a development because here we have all this
> wonderful technology so that these kids can learn, and
> [they] have all the tools at their disposal so that they can do
> the very best job they can, and then we have this very small
> percentage . . . of kids who dispense knowledge of how to
> compromise the network.

Candice has always tried to communicate clear consequences for any discipline infractions and to follow through with the particular penalties. However, computer infractions have increasingly placed a burden on her. She now has to type names and grades rather than downloading them from the computer. She estimates that what normally took three minutes now takes three to six hours. When students misuse the technology, it is time-consuming for her to catch culprits and the penalty (no access to computers) affects students' learning. Such a compromise is difficult for her.

> I had to go up to a level of discipline on the computer net-
> work that I've never had to do before. And it seemed like I
> spent an awful a lot of time tracking down this behavior
> this year. So I've decided to go to a new system next year,
> which is that every kid and their parent will sign a contract
> of behavior . . . And essentially [if] you get one warning,
> you lose rights to your account for two weeks and then af-
> ter that, [for] the rest of the semester with possible other
> sanctions. Now the problem with that, of course, is that at
> Futurist School, it is impossible for a student to pass their
> classes without access to the computers . . . So it's been
> really hard for me to come up with this thing . . . but the
> level of seriousness of the offenses has become so hard.

The most serious examples of computer infractions in the school have been computer hacking and death threats on computers. What is so astonishing to Candice is that "the level of morality that [she] would like to see isn't even remotely there." She found a newspaper clipping about two students in another district who were "brought up on felony charges for doing much of the same stuff that these kids are doing." Her point in reading the article to her students was to emphasize the seriousness of the charges. She was unprepared for the students' reaction.

> But you know what they focused on? They focused on
> "How could it be theft? Isn't it criminal trespass?" See, they
> didn't even focus on the fact that these were felony charges.
> That was the point! . . . I said, "Wait a minute. You're miss-
> ing the point of my reading this. The point is it's a felony.
> Doesn't matter whether it's trespass or theft. And there are
> lifetime repercussions of this."

Clearly, students must be able to count on help from teachers to develop morally as well as intellectually and socially.

Candice and her colleagues are aware that the traditional teaching role of delivering subject content to students—something a computer can do well—is far from adequate in meeting the state goal to create schools where students can become healthy and productive citizens of the 21st century. Computers are equally inadequate in preparing adolescents socially and morally for life in a complex, democratic society. Teaching for the holistic development of students involves modeling social/emotional maturity and sound, ethical judgment.

> If you talk about healthy and productive citizens, a healthy person is someone who has self-discipline, who respects themselves and others, thinks before they act, is sensitive to what goes on around them, and is willing to accept responsibility for what they do no matter what the consequences are. And if they've thought before they've acted, then they kind of weighed out what most of the consequences are going to be for their action. We definitely try to do that.

The limitations of computers

Computers are now a fact of life in American schools although accessibility and instructional use vary widely. The introduction of computers into classrooms has brought both blessings and burdens to both teachers and students. However, the most serious problems facing schools are not going to be solved by quick access to vast amounts of information made easy with computers. Intellectually, students need teachers to help them learn to evaluate the credibility of information, sift and analyze information, think critically, and make or assess judgments. Computers are impotent in solving social/emotional problems teachers face: conflict and anger, social inequalities, alienated adolescents, unmotivated students, and unacceptable behaviors. Teaching relies on social skills necessary for developing good relationships and negotiating conflicts. Additionally, good human relationships and the resolution of difficult or complex social situations require moral judgments.

Computers are unable to address the lack of morals that allow some students to hurt or burden others directly or indirectly. Students need help and practice to learn respect, sensitivity, self-discipline, and responsibility. In schools, the kind of intellectual, social, and moral development that adolescents need, especially in a technology-driven culture, must come from teachers who themselves are critical thinkers and who demonstrate the respect and responsibility they hope to instill in their students.

Students in the 21st century could continue to learn without school computers if they had to. After all, most children in the world do not yet have access to computers in school and many readers of this paper did not have computers as students. However, children need guidance from teachers in order to develop intellectually, socially, and morally. The teachers may be parents, professional teachers, or some other respected adult. Such teachers are even more indispensable as children face a future of technologies that will continue to change cultures around the globe, and an increasingly complex future that will require socially compassionate and morally responsible decisions.

Organizations and Websites

The editors have compiled the following list of organizations concerned with the issues debated in this book. The descriptions are derived from materials provided by the organizations. All have publications or information available for interested readers. The list was compiled on the date of publication of the present volume; the information provided here may change. Be aware that many organizations take several weeks or longer to respond to inquiries, so allow as much time as possible.

Alliance for Childhood

PO Box 444, College Park, MD 20741
(301) 779-1033
website: www.allianceforchildhood.net

The Alliance for Childhood is a partnership of individuals and organizations committed to fostering and respecting each child's right to a healthy, developmentally appropriate childhood. The alliance opposes the use of computers in early childhood education and elementary schools. The organization's position statement, "Children and Computers: A Call to Action," is available on its website, as is its report on computers and children, *Fool's Gold: A Critical Look at Computers and Childhood.*

Benton Foundation

1625 K St. NW, 11th Floor, Washington, DC 20006
(202) 638-5770
websites: www.benton.org • www.connectforkids.org
www.digitaldividenetwork.org

The Benton Foundation works to demonstrate the value of digital media for solving social problems. It supports children's increased access to technology for education. The foundation's Digital Divide Network works to reduce the digital divide between those who have access to computer and Internet technology and those who do not. The foundation publishes a newsletter, a collection of articles entitled *Effective Language for Discussing Early Childhood Education and Policy,* and the report *The Learning Connection: Schools in the Information Age.*

The Children's Partnership

2000 P St. NW, Suite 330, Washington, DC 20036-6904
(202) 429-0033
website: www.childrenspartnership.org

The Children's Partnership is a national nonprofit organization whose mission is to inform leaders and the public about the needs of America's 70 million children, and to engage them in ways that benefit children. Through its Children and Technology program the partnership explores how the Internet and related technologies can best serve children. The organization is involved with a $6 million initiative in California to build community computer centers in eleven low-income communities. The alliance publishes a series of *Next Generation* reports that deal with computers and children, as well as the report *The Parents' Guide to the Information Superhighway.*

Department of Education, Office of Education Technology (OET)
400 Maryland Ave. SW, Washington, DC 20202
(800) USA-LEARN
website: www.ed.gov/technology

The OET develops national educational technology policy and implements this policy through department-wide educational technology programs. The office assisted with the Falling Through the Net project that studied the digital divide from 1994 to 2000 as well as the Web-Based Education Commission, which released its final report in 2000 (the websites for both these programs are discussed below). Reports available at the office's website include *eLearning: Putting a World-Class Education at the Fingertips of All Children, Internet Access in Public Schools and Classrooms: 1994–1999,* and *An Educator's Guide to Evaluating the Use of Technology in Schools and Classrooms.*

Digital Promise Project
c/o The Century Foundation, 41 East 70th St., New York, NY 10021
(212) 535-4441
website: www.digitalpromise.org

Digital Promise's goal is to unlock the potential of the Internet and other new information technologies for education. It funds efforts to train teachers in the use of information technology and to digitize educational resources. The *Digital Promise Report* is available for download on the organization's website.

Educause
1150 18th St. NW, Suite 1010, Washington, DC 20036
(202) 872-4200
website: www.educause.edu

Educause is a nonprofit association of higher education institutions, corporations, and other related groups that works to advance higher education by promoting the intelligent use of information technology. It holds seminars and conferences on the effective implementation of technology in higher education and supports legislation that facilitates this process. Its publications include *Educause Quarterly* and many books, such as *The Internet and the University* and *Technology-Enhanced Teaching and Learning: Leading and Supporting the Transformation on Your Campus.*

International Society for Technology in Education (ISTE)
480 Charnelton St., Eugene, OR 97401-2626
(800) 336-5191
e-mail: iste@iste.org • website: www.iste.org

ISTE is a nonprofit professional organization with a worldwide membership of leaders and potential leaders in educational technology. It is dedicated to promoting appropriate uses of information technology to support and improve learning, teaching, and administration in K–12 education and teacher education. Its National Educational Technology Standards project works to develop national standards for educational uses of technology that facilitate school improvement in the United States. It publishes the report *Research on Technology in Education* and the book *National Educational Standards for Teachers—Preparing Teachers to Use Technology.*

The Sapio Institute
PO Box 983, Southeastern, PA 19399-0983
(610) 296-5623
website: www.sapioinstitute.org

The Sapio Institute is a nonprofit, e-learning research and professional development organization whose focus is to study the implementation, effectiveness, and impact of e-learning or online learning. The organization believes that online instructional systems have the potential to become powerful delivery channels for expanding human learning and knowledge. Members of the institute have published a variety of research articles in academic journals.

Websites

Computers for Learning (CFL)
www.computers.fed.gov

CFL is a federal program that transfers excess federal computer equipment to schools and educational nonprofit organizations, giving special consideration to those with the greatest need. The CFL website helps connect registered schools and educational nonprofit organizations with available government computer equipment.

EDSITEment
edsitement.neh.gov

The EDSITEment website was launched in 1997 by the National Endowment for the Humanities, the Council of the Great City Schools, WorldCom Foundation and the National Trust for the Humanities. Its purpose is to aid teachers, students, and parents searching for high-quality material on the Internet in the subject areas of literature and language arts, foreign languages, art and culture, and history and social studies.

Falling Through the Net
www.digitaldivide.gov

This site was established by the Commerce Department's National Telecommunications and Information Administration (NTIA) to inform the public of the federal government's activities regarding Americans' access to the Internet and other information technologies. The site contains the reports *Falling Through the Net: Defining the Digital Divide, Falling Through the Net: Toward Digital Inclusion,* and *A Nation Online: How Americans Are Expanding Their Use Of the Internet.*

Web-Based Education Commission
www.hpcnet.org/webcommission

The commission was established by Congress in 1999 to develop policy recommendations geared toward maximizing the educational promise of the Internet for pre-K, elementary, middle, secondary, and postsecondary education learners. The commission's final report, *The Power of the Internet for Learning: Moving from Promise to Practice*, is available on its website, as are the statements of over two hundred individuals and organizations who testified before the commission between July and November 2000.

Bibliography

Books

Alison Armstrong and Charles Casement — *The Child and the Machine: How Computers Put Our Children's Education at Risk.* Beltsville, MD: Robins Lane Press, 2000.

Jay Blanchard, ed. — *Education Computing in the Schools: Technology, Communication, and Literacy.* New York: Haworth Press, 1999.

John D. Bradsford, Ann L. Brown, and Rodney R. Cocking, eds. — *How People Learn: Brain, Mind, Experience, and School.* Washington, DC: National Academy Press, 1999.

Larry Cuban — *Oversold and Underused: Computers in the Classroom.* Cambridge: Harvard University Press, 2001.

G. David Garson, ed. — *Social Dimensions of Information Technology: Issues for the New Millennium.* Hershey: Ideas Group, 2000.

Paul S. Goodman, ed. — *Technology-Enhanced Learning: Opportunities for Change.* Mahwah, NJ: L. Erlbaum, 2002.

David H. Jonassen et al. — *Computers as Mindtools for Schools: Engaging Critical Thinking.* Upper Saddle River, NJ: Merrill, 2000.

David J. McArthur and Matthew W. Lewis — *Untangling the Web: Applications of the Internet and Other Information Technologies to Higher Learning.* Santa Monica: RAND, 1998.

Gary R. Morrison and Deborah L. Lowther — *Integrating Computer Technology into the Classroom.* Upper Saddle River, NJ: Merrill/Prentice-Hall, 2002.

Matthew Pittinsky — *The Wired Tower: Perspectives on the Impact of the Internet in Higher Education.* Upper Saddle River, NJ: Financial Times/Prentice-Hall, 2002.

Clifford Stoll — *High-Tech Heretic: Why Computers Don't Belong in the Classroom and Other Reflections by a Computer Contrarian.* New York: Doubleday, 1999.

David Trend — *Welcome to Cyberschool: Education at the Crossroads in the Information Age.* Lanham, MD: Rowman & Littlefield, 2001.

Christopher R. Wolfe, ed. — *Learning and Teaching on the World Wide Web.* San Diego: Academic, 2001.

Periodicals

Larry Cuban — "System Crash," *Boston Globe,* November 25, 2001.

Lisa Guersey — "O.K., Schools Are Wired, Now What?" *New York Times,* January 9, 2000.

Katie Hafner   "Schools and Computers: Debate Heats Up," *New York Times*, October 5, 2000.

Dan Johnson   "The Cyber Children Have Arrived," *Futurist*, September 2001.

Doug Johnson   "All That Glitters," *School Library Journal*, December 2000.

Katy Kelley et al.   "False Promise," *U.S. News & World Report*, September 25, 2000.

Ellin Martens   "A Laptop for Every Kid," *Time*, May 1, 2000.

Kelly McCarthy   "Techno Tots," *Psychology Today*, January/February 2001.

Thomas J. McCarthy   "Report from Four-Year-Olds," *America*, March 12, 2001.

Sally McGrane   "Creating a Generation of Slouchers," *New York Times*, January 4, 2001.

Bonnie Rothman   "A Day in the Life of the Wired School," *New York Times*,
Morris   October 5, 2000.

Amelia Newcomb   "What? A School Without Computers?" *Christian Science Monitor*, November 2, 1999.

Rachel Hartigan Shea   "Special Report: E-Learning Guide," *U.S. News & World*
and Ulrich Boser   *Report*, October 15, 2001.

William C. Symonds   "Special Report: Wired Schools," *Business Week*, September 25, 2000.

Jennifer Tanaka   "An Extreme Reaction?" *Newsweek*, September 25, 2000.

Chris Taylor et al.   "So Close and Yet So Far," *Time*, December 4, 2000.

Bob Thompson   "Learning to Be Wired," *Washington Post*, September 16, 2001.

Time   "Digital Divide," December 4, 2000.

Andrew Trotter   "Effectiveness of Computers Still Open to Question," *Education Week*, September 20, 2000.

Lawrence Williams   "Fool's Gold or Hidden Treasure: Are Computers Stifling Creativity?" *Journal of Education Policy*, September/October 2001.

Index

administration, automating, 20
adolescents, 70–71, 102
 see also students
advertising, 38
after-school programs, 82–83
Alliance for Childhood, 73
American Schools Directory, 33
Amirault, Chris, 79, 81
Applebee, A.N., 62
Apple Computer, 9, 38
Armstrong, Alison, 37
artificial intelligence, 14
Atkinson, R., 22
Audubon Middle School, 52–53

Ball, Deborah, 35
Bank Street College, 24
Barnes, Susan B., 85
Barrett, G., 88
Becker, Henry Jay, 39–40
Becker, Sue, 78–79
bell curve, 44–45
Belvedere system, 27
Benioff, Marc, 82–83
Bennett, Frederick, 93
Bennetts, Leslie, 49
books, 87–89
Bridges Beacon, 83
Brynjoltsson, Erik, 95
Building a Digital Workforce: Confronting the
 Crisis (National Policy Association), 10
Burnett, J. Dale, 44
Bush, George W., 10
Bush, Vannevar, 26

calculators, 59–60
California Learning Assessment Study
 (CLAS), 42–43
Camelot Elementary School, 50–51
Caprio, Michael J., 54
Carnegie Mellon University, 96–97
Casement, Charles, 37
Cassidy, Jack, 80
chat rooms, 70–71
Chestnut Ridge School District, 17–18
Children's Partnership, 66
Cincinnati Bell, 80–81
Cisco Systems, 80
class size. See teachers
Classtalk, 30
Clinton, Bill, 9, 90

cloning, 15
Clough, Michael P., 56
Collinson, Vivienne, 101
community-based school projects,
 32–34, 51–52
computer-assisted instruction (CAI)
 advantages and disadvantages of, 86–88
 changing role of teachers under, 98–99
 computers serving as tutors through,
 96–98
 connecting classrooms to the
 community with, 32–34
 considering rationales for using, 63–64
 cultural divide and, 81–84
 efficiency in, 13
 electronic communities and, 33
 as enhancing learning, 22–23
 failure of, 85–86
 funding for other programs vs.
 funding for, 16, 17–18
 future of, 99–100
 government funding and support for,
 9–10, 90
 human approach to education vs.,
 75–76
 as hurting academic performance,
 43–44
 is not developmentally advantageous
 to children, 73–74
 learning from real-world problems
 through, 23–26
 makes learning fun, 49–55
 movement for, 9–10
 opportunities for teacher-student
 communication with, 29–31
 questioning reasons for using, 90
 research on. See research
 as retarding conceptual understanding
 of subject, 59–63
 scaffolding technologies with, 26–29
 socioeconomic divisions and, 78–81
 student individualization through, 13
 taking a moderate position on, 56
 teacher interaction missing with,
 43–44
 teacher learning through, 33–36
 teacher vs. computer interaction with
 students and, 95
 traditional literacy skills and, 90–92
 tutoring environment provided with,
 31–32

undermines serious study, 57–59
see also computers; Internet; software;
    teachers
computers
    administrative purposes of, 20–21
    advertising exaggerating promises of,
        38
    age-appropriate guidelines for using,
        68–71
    as changing culture, 104
    ethical use of, 109–11
    in the homes, 37–38
    impact of, on workplace opportunities,
        14, 66
    importance of childhood over, 74–75
    increased use of, 66–67
    introduction of personal, 9
    limitations of, 112
    negative impact of home, 43
    parents lacking skills in, 67
    positive impact from, 67–68
    skewed priorities over, 18–19
    social isolation with, 107
    used by girls, 71–72
    ways to improve education instead of
        using, 21
    see also computer-assisted instruction;
        Internet; software
Computer-Supported Intentional
    Learning Environment (CSILE), 30
constructivist learning theory, 57, 102
Corporate IT, 79
CoVis Project, 25–26, 28, 31
Cuban, Larry, 76
cybercrime, 110–11

Davenport, Gloriana, 86
Delano Optional School, 51
Delgado, Manuel, 82
Dertouzos, Michael, 11
DeVaney, A., 104
Dewey, John, 76, 102
DiBianca, Suzanne, 83
digital divide, 78–81

education
    after-school programs and, 82–83
    computers have not improved, 94–95
    entertainment and, 58–59
    improving, with human relationships
        vs. with technology, 75–76
    improving, without computers, 21
    lack of change in, 12–13
    recommendations for, 77
    warning on failure of, 9
    see also computer-assisted instruction;
        teachers
Educational Testing Service (ETS), 43

Eisner, E.W., 62
Elastic Media, 86
Ellul, Jacques, 85
e-mail
    with Olympic athletes, 53
    pen pals, 50–51, 67
engineering, genetic, 15
    see also technology
Etheridge, Will, 52

Fairbairn, Joyce, 91
Fayette, Alabama, 51–52
Fayette Middle School, 51–52
film, digital, 86–87
Florida A&M University, 39
Florida State University, 39
*Frames of Mind: The Theory of Multiple
    Intelligence* (Gardner), 45

Gardner, Howard, 12, 45
Gates, Elaine, 54–55
GenScope Project, 28–29
geography, 47–48
Gibson, Stephanie, 88
girls, 71–72
Global Lab, 24–25
Goleman, D., 102–103
Goodman, Danny, 90–91
Granby High School, 53–54
Gulf Coast High School, 54

hacking, 110–11
Halo, Tiffany, 83–84
Harms, Mark, 81
Harrison, Tom, 91
Hartwig, Eric, 81, 82
Hemrick, Christine, 80
Hewlett–Packard, 80
Hitt, Lorin, 95
Hutcher, Peter, 21
Hynes, William, 46
hypertext, 87–90

IBM (International Business Machines), 9
imagination, 74–75
imaging technologies, 14
Indiana University, 36
information technologists
    digital divide and, 79
    training of, 80
    see also teachers
innumeracy, 60
integrated learning systems (ILSs), 39–40
Internet
    digital divide and, 78
    vs. exploring information locally,
        17–18
    government funding for, 9–10
    innovative projects with, 53–54

misinformation on, 13–14
schools do not have a duty to provide,
   21
teacher communities on, 34–35
training for, 17
using real-life objects instead of, 18–19
see also computer-assisted instruction;
   computers

Jagmin, Karen, 53
Jasper Adventuremaker, 29
Jasper Woodbury Problem Solving
   Series, 24
Jeannero, Susan, 82

Khirallah, Diane Rezendes, 78
Kids as Global Scientists (KGS), 33
Knowledge Forum, 30
Kohl, Herbert, 45
Kuntz, Debbie, 50

labs, computer, 19
   see also science; software
Lakeland High School, 96
Lampert, Magdalene, 35
Landow, B.P., 88
Langer, J.A., 62
Lawrence High School, 96
LEAF (Local Education Advancement
   Foundation), 52
learning. *See* education
Learning Through Collaborative
   Visualization. *See* CoVis Project
Levin, James, 34
Lewiston, Idaho, 50–51
Link Community School, 78–79, 83–84
Lipe, Cathy, 80
literacy
   computer, 88–90
   gap, 88–90
   importance of traditional, 90–92

mathematics, 24
   calculators and, 59–60
   computer use having a negative
      impact on scores for, 43
   scaffolding technologies with, 26–27, 28
Memphis, Tennessee, 51
Menlo-Atherton High School, 81–82
Microsoft, 38
Middle School Mathematics Through
   Applications Project (MMAP), 26
Miller, Larry, 44
Milwaukee, Wisconsin, 52–53
Minnesota Technology Demonstration
   Project, 39
multimedia, 51–52, 54–55

Naples, Florida, 54

National Commission on Excellence in
   Education, 9
National Policy Association, 10
National Research Council (NRC), 22
National Science Board (NSB), 11
Nation at Risk, A (National Commission
   on Excellence in Education), 9
Negroponte, Nicholas, 86, 87
Networking Academy, 82
Noble, Douglas, 40
No Child Left Behind Act (2002), 10
Norfolk, Virginia, 53–54
North Central Regional Educational
   Laboratory, 36
NovaNet Learning, Inc., 96

Olson, Joanne K., 56

Papert, S., 87
parents
   involvement of, in child's education, 68
   lack of computer skills and, 67
   setting age–appropriate guidelines for
      computer use, 68–71
   wanting computers for their children,
      37–38
Pearlman, R., 61
pen pals (electronic), 50–51, 67
   see also e-mail
philanthropy, 80–83
physical education, 54–55
plagiarism, 110
Popp, Kathy, 17, 21
Postman, Neil, 58, 86, 104
Powell, Colin, 83
Project GLOBE (Global Learning and
   Observation to Benefit the
   Environment), 25

Ratsch, Peggy, 18
research
   drawbacks of standardized testing for,
      44–45
   lack of critical writing from, 42
   mixed and contradictory results in,
      38–40
   need for additional, 11
   problems with, 40–42

Salesforce.com Inc., 82–83
San Jose Mercury News (newspaper),
   42–43
scaffolds, 26–29
schools. *See* computer-assisted
   instruction; education
science
   computer labs replacing labs for,
      19–20
   creative process and, 74–75

learning, through real-life context,
24–26
need for serious study on, 57
scaffolding technologies for, 27, 28–29
technology impedes literacy in, 60–61
using real-life objects vs. Internet for,
18–19
Shellito, Richard, 81
Sherlock Project, 32
SMART (Special Multimedia Arenas for
Refining Thinking) Challenge Series, 29
software
learning out of context with, 47–48
mathematics, 26–27
science, 28–29
visualization and modeling, 23
Starr, Paul, 9
Steiner, Rudolf, 76
STELLA modeling environment, 28
Stoll, Clifford, 10, 16
students
attitudes of, on computers, 40–41
communication with teachers and
peers by, 29–31
computer use fosters school interest in,
49–55
cooperative participation with teachers
by, 34
teacher interaction with, 43–44, 95
technology furthering study on, 14–15
Student/Teacher Achievement Ratio
(STAR) Project, 46
Suppes, Patrick, 22

TAAS (Texas Assessment of Academic
Skills), 96
Taft IT Academy, 80–81
Talbott, Steve, 87
Tapscott, Don, 42
TeacherOutreach.org, 81
Teacher Professional Development
Institute, 35
teachers
class size and, 46–47
communication with students by, 29–31
computerized education changing role
of, 98–99
computer literacy requirements of, 89
computers as tutors replacing, 96–98
computers providing opportunities for
learning by, 33–36
as guiding moral development, 109–12
holistic role of, 101–103, 112
impact of computer knowledge by,
43–44
interaction with students by, 95

lack of superb, 93–94
making data meaningful to students,
104–105
money for technology vs. money for
hiring, 11, 17
prioritizing computers over, 19
role of, in education, 62
role of, in implementation of research
studies, 41–42
as teaching social skills, 107–109, 112
as teaching students how to access and
judge information, 105–107
technology coordinators replacing, 21
technology training for, 94
technology
altering education, 15–16
examining need for, 64–65
teacher training in, 94
technology coordinators, 21
Technology Literacy Fund, 9–10
teenagers. *See* adolescents; students
television, 92
as changing culture, 104
as endangering children's thinking,
107
entertainment and, 58–59
testing, standardized
research and, 44–45
tutorial programs and, 96, 97
toddlers, 69
Tokyo Institute of Technology, 41
TriFit, 55
Trull, Melanie, 52
Turkle, Sherry, 13, 18, 77
Turner High School, 96
tutoring, 31–32, 96–98

Victoria Foundation, 83–84
videoconferencing, 50
videos
learning through real-life problems
with, 24
teacher learning with, 35–36
virtual reality, 14
Voyage of the Mimi, The (educational
software), 24

Wenglinsky, Harold, 43
Werner, Cary, 53
Where in the World Is Carmen Sandiego?
(educational software), 47
Where in Time Is Carmen Sandiego?
(educational software), 47–48
Williams, Lynn, 51

Youth Leadership Initiative, 53–54